RACHEL'S HOPE

RACHEL'S HOPE

CAROLE GIFT PAGE

Jeremy Books

5624 Lincoln Drive Edina, Minnesota 55436

5624 Lincoln Drive Edina, Minnesota 55436

Chapter One

Rachel's first impression was that Dr. Bernard Oberg's waiting room was like an oversized walk-in closet, neatly camouflaged with nursery bric-a-brac and semigloss paint. The room was small and narrow with baby blue walls, bare except for an occasional pastel drawing of a child hugging a pink blanket or clutching a teddy bear. The drawings were signed simply Muriel, with no last name.

Rachel approached the nurse's desk wondering what difference it all made—the walls, the paintings and Muriel, whoever she was. There were too many other things to wonder about now. Thoughts and questions were buzzing inside her skull like bees, and it was horribly irritating. *What does a woman do who might be pregnant—a woman who is convinced that having a baby is unthinkable, a tragedy?*

Rachel had already wondered about this possibility, for she wasn't sure how long. She just knew that the idea had grown stronger, more pressing and more probable than before. Realizing at last that something had to be done, she had gone to the telephone directory and selected a number—the number of a Long Beach obstetrician, a random choice—and dialed. She had made this appointment for Monday afternoon, October 15th, at four o'clock.

"Excuse me, I'm Mrs. Webber, Rachel Webber," she explained to the preoccupied receptionist-nurse.

She realized that she sounded apologetic; she hated that sound in her voice. Unconsciously, she patted the side of her skirt, straightening it, while the young woman in starched white looked up from whatever she was doing to offer a smooth, professional smile. She was pretty, Rachel noted, with her blonde hair swept back in a meticulous, efficient sort of way—the kind of controlled beauty one expected of a nurse.

"Oh, yes, Mrs. Webber," she replied crisply. "I have a form I'd like you to fill out."

"I brought the specimen you asked for."

"Fine. Why don't you have a seat?"

"How long will it take? I mean, can I find out right away?"

Again the nurse flashed her easy, detached smile. "With the tests we have now, Mrs. Webber, we can obtain the results almost immediately. The lab is right next door, so if you will just take a seat, the doctor will see you and give you a report in about half an hour."

Rachel Webber slipped into a vacant chair by the door, her face clouded, expressionless. She set her purse at her feet and leaned back, crossing her legs at the ankle. Then she gazed ahead at nothing in particular, at the pastel child clutching his teddy bear, at the blue wall—and breathed deeply, willing herself to relax.

Lately, she reflected somberly, it seemed impossible to relax. She could not manage to read through an entire article in *Good Housekeeping*; her thoughts wandered when she played Mantovani or Burt Bacharach on the stereo. She could not even concentrate on Taylor Caldwell's *Glory and the Lightning*, although it was a novel she wanted to read. The simple fact was that Rachel could not force out of her mind the idea that she might

8

be pregnant. She could not afford to be pregnant now. After all, a pregnancy would affect her whole life, everything.

Today Rachel would find out for sure. She didn't want to know, but she would know. In a half hour someone would come and tell her the future course of her life— just like that, the whole future course. How ironic could you get?

For the first time since entering the room, she dared to glance around. A young couple, probably just teenagers, sat close to each other on an orange vinyl couch. The girl flipped through the pages of a baby magazine; the boy, studying the walls and ceiling with an intense concentration, tapped his fingers nervously on the arm of the couch.

"Look at this beautiful nursery furniture, Jeff," Rachel heard the girl say. "Wouldn't you love to have that for the baby?"

The boy glanced at the picture, grunted, and stared back at the ceiling. "Your mother doesn't have room in her house for that kind of stuff," he answered hoarsely. "We'll be lucky to squeeze in a crib."

Another woman, dark-haired and plain—perhaps in her early 30s, like Rachel—sat serenely reading a gothic novel. Rachel couldn't help staring. The woman was huge. She was obviously due any moment. Rachel wondered if she had been that large when she carried Brian. She couldn't have been, but she didn't remember. It had been 13 years ago.

The woman looked up from her novel, catching Rachel's stare. They exchanged quick, embarrassed smiles and turned their eyes away.

Rachel had to admit that there was something fascinating about a woman who could sit patiently reading when at any moment all of her life forces could be called into action for the delivery of a child. After all, wasn't childbirth an awesome, turbulent experience, something for which a woman had to prepare her entire mind and body—right down to the nerve-endings? And when the thing started and the waves and turbulence swept over her, she would realize that no amount of preparation was quite enough. At least, Rachel had found it that way when Brian was born.

But the woman across from Rachel appeared totally untroubled, as if she were quite ready to accept whatever pain or discomfort she would have to bear. Rachel envied her, for rarely could she herself sit back calmly and let things come as they would and pass over her. Somehow, it was too important for Rachel to be in control, in the driver's seat, steering her life the way she felt it ought to go. Not that she always steered so well!

Rachel shifted uncomfortably in her chair, willing the time away. It occurred to her that she should pray for a negative report so that she could get out of this cracker-box office and forget her ridiculous fear that she might be pregnant.

But what if she were pregnant? What then? Jerry would have a fit. He would blame her. He was so involved in—in other things now. One thing their marriage didn't need was a baby! *Please, dear Lord, don't let it be*, she willed silently. *Don't let it be*!

Rachel realized that she was still holding the form the nurse had given her. She searched her purse for a pen and scribbled into the blank spaces the information requested. Name. Address. Telephone number. Insurance. She couldn't remember who carried their insurance. She would have to check with Jerry.

She laid the form aside and glanced at her reflection in the oval mirror on the opposite wall, noting with satisfaction that her makeup was correct. She had good eyes, she was confident of that. Of course, her brows were too dark and thick to be pretty, and her mouth was perhaps too wide. But her medium-length brown hair had been done that morning. Jenny from the Carousel Beauty Salon did her hair each week, making the curls fall softly onto Rachel's forehead and caress her cheekbones.

Rachel conceded that she was no classic beauty, but Jerry considered her pretty and still young. (Could 32 be old?) Long ago he told her she had the grace of a madonna. He said no one walked with as much grace as she.

Rachel smiled inadvertently. Did Jerry really say things like that once? It must have been some other lifetime, some other Rachel—the old Rachel. The girl she was when they were married. The high school girl who could hardly wait for graduation, who, less than two weeks later, became Mrs. Jerry Webber in one of the gaudy little wedding chapels in Las Vegas. That girl had been gone for a long time, Rachel admitted.

Waiting for the nurse to call her name, there was little for Rachel to do but to think and to remember. So she sat back, nearly succeeding in her attempt to relax, and permitted the reels of memory to spin through her mind like old film clips.

Thirteen years ago Brian was born. She and Jerry had been married only a year, and Jerry still had another year before he would receive his engineering degree from California State University at Long Beach. Rachel had to give up her typing job to take care of Brian, and Jerry took a part-time job at night to pay the rent on their small Long Beach apartment.

Those early days of adjustment were difficult, to say the least. Life was easier before their marriage or even during that first year, for there were the art lectures and travel films at the college, the pizza parties with other students on Friday nights, and the Saturday drives to Solvang or San Diego. There were the walks through Knott's Berry Farm, with popcorn and paper cups of boysenberry juice balanced in their hands as they peered through the smudged, ancient storefront windows of that lovely ghost town.

Such excursions were sweet interludes in their tedium, inexpensive activities that she and Jerry enjoyed together. But after Brian came, it seemed that she and Jerry rarely saw each other. He would spend the day in class or else at the library studying. Sometimes he came home for dinner before rushing off to his job at the garage, but just as often he grabbed a sandwich somewhere, and she wouldn't see him until he collapsed into bed beside her long after midnight.

Perhaps her schedule wasn't so hectic as Jerry's, but she was just as tired—and often depressed. Brian was a fussy, demanding baby who kept her constantly on the run. He fretted when he was alone and was continuously into things; yet he screamed when she put him in the playpen so that she could relax in the tub or read a magazine.

Perhaps it wouldn't have seemed so bad if she could have shared with Jerry some of her daily frustrations with Brian. But Jerry was always busy, always preoccupied with his studies or his work. On weekends, when he was home, he parked himself before the TV set, watching football or baseball, or else he caught up on his sleep. In either case, Rachel was still forced to chase after Brian to keep him from disturbing his father.

Things improved after Jerry graduated. He found a good position in the aerospace industry and quit his evening job. He had regular hours and was able to spend more time at home. Brian was older, too, and more settled, and he began to look forward to the hour before dinner when he could roughhouse with Daddy.

They were finally able to save a little money to buy some of the things they wanted. They moved to a nicer apartment several blocks from the old one. The new place was larger and impressive, in one of Southern California's modern, luxurious apartment complexes, surrounded by palm trees and tropical shrubs. There was a swimming pool in the sprawling, center patio area, and colored lights abounded everywhere, providing an artificial—even brackish—impression of opulence.

Rachel would have preferred buying a home of their own, but Jerry had a thousand reasons why buying a home would be impractical. High interest rates. Inflation. A precarious economy. Then, his main excuse had been the instability of the aerospace industry. He didn't want to get saddled with a heavy mortgage when who knew what tomorrow would bring. Better to remain without ties, he said. Remain flexible, ready to pull up stakes, if necessary, without the usual trauma of uprooting a settled household.

They had lived in that same apartment now for 10 years. Sometimes, particularly on Sunday afternoons, they would go for a drive and stop to look at model homes. They would walk through the professionally decorated rooms, praising a painting or commenting on the subtle greens in a shag rug or the exquisite pattern of the wallpaper. They would survey the fine assortment of family rooms and dens, play rooms and bonus rooms that many of the homes boasted. It was at such model homes that Rachel had seen the large walk-in closets (nearly as large as this very office) and the master bedrooms that were practically a home in themselves. On such excursions, she and Jerry would discuss the possibility of buying a home. And Jerry would say again, "One of these days—maybe . . ." Lately though, she reflected, he didn't even say that.

Somehow, lately, Jerry seemed to be pulling away from Brian and her. His life seemed to be increasingly disconnected from theirs. Of course, they had gone their separate ways to some extent for years. But this was something else, something more.

Again the suspicions nagged her. What about Jerry? What was he doing? What was going on? Or was she being crazy to wonder about him when there was really no reason? What was wrong with her that she doubted her own husband? God forgive her suspicions!

Defensively Rachel reminded herself that, no matter what the problems now, *once* her marriage had been good. At least, until—when was it? When did she and Jerry really begin to grow apart?

There was only one answer to that question. It was after she met Marlene Benson. When was that? Five years ago? That long? Yes. Brian was about eight. Marlene moved into an apartment downstairs. She was alone. Her husband had been killed four or five years before in an explosion in the factory where he worked. They had no children.

In spite of her loss, Marlene was a generous, wonderfully open person. She had a quality of love about her that drew Rachel. Marlene was older than Rachel and looked older still, for she wore no makeup and kept her dark hair in a loose bun at the nape of her neck. Marlene was large-boned and perhaps a few pounds overweight. There was almost a gangliness about her, as if no matter where she shopped, she would never be able to find clothing that fit properly. Rachel's affection for Marlene grew quickly, for it seemed that in this one plain, lovely woman Rachel could find the sympathetic understanding of a mother, big sister, and friend.

Rachel missed the influence of older people on her life. Her parents had died in an automobile accident on the Hollywood Freeway during her senior year of high school. Jerry's parents lived in a small town in Ohio, so Rachel rarely saw them. Only the exchange of perfunctory monthly letters kept them in touch. So Marlene met a need. She and Rachel became close friends.

Rachel discovered soon enough that Marlene had fascinating opinions about many things—what it meant to be a woman, a Christian woman; what her responsibilities were to herself and to others; what her relationship ought to be to God. Marlene related these opinions one afternoon while they had coffee in Rachel's apartment.

"When my husband died, I felt like I had hit rock bottom," Marlene confided. "That's when I knew Christ was real. He took me by the hand and said, 'Honey, it's all right. You're going to be okay. Just walk with Me.'"

"Wow," Rachel had retorted. "Might as well have asked you to walk on water or something."

"No, Rachel," Marlene replied with a smile. "I don't imagine I could do that. But what He asked *was* possible. Really. Many people are doing it all the time."

"Are you saying that you're trying to be perfect?" quizzed Rachel. "That would kill me off as quickly as anything. It's hard enough just plodding through each day."

"No, I'm not saying that," Marlene assured her. "But following Jesus is so simple, so beautiful. Once you dig into the Word of God and let the Holy Spirit get hold of your life, you discover that God's Son is a real person. Not just a man in history. Not just a pie-in-the-sky religion. Rachel, honey, Jesus got off that cross a long time ago, and He's not lying in that tomb anymore. He's alive, He's God, and He loves me."

"It sounds fantastic," Rachel replied. "But definitely not simple."

Even now, sitting stiffly, impatiently in the doctor's waiting room, Rachel could recall the words Marlene had spoken to her—the quiet, direct way she explained the plan of salvation, the blood atonement of Jesus Christ, His resurrection, His willingness to live in the heart of the believer and the constant working of His Spirit through the yielded Christian.

Rachel's amazement had turned to curiosity, then to hunger. Here was Christianity as she had never heard it before—beautiful, powerful, capable of giving life a meaning she had always wished for but never dreamed possible. It involved so many things she was familiar with—Jesus of Nazareth, Christmas and Easter, church attendance, prayer. Things everyone knew about. But then why hadn't anyone told her that religion was just the periphery of the matter, that the nucleus, the center

16

of it all, was Christ? And that the purpose of living was to love and glorify God by yielding one's life constantly, moment by moment, to the Person of Jesus Christ?

Marlene prayed with Rachel one day and led her like a child into saving faith in Jesus Christ. For a long while after that, Rachel felt the wonder of innocence and the amazement of childhood in her blood again. She was free, clean. Even her daily routine took on purpose. It had all been so good.

It was still good, Rachel noted silently, but things were different now. She couldn't deny that some of the sparkle was gone. The sheen of her brand-new faith had worn thin, and faded with the passing of months and years.

It wasn't entirely Rachel's fault, she reasoned coolly. If only her faith hadn't become a wedge in her marriage; if only Jerry shared her faith instead of resenting it; if only he would help encourage Brian's faith by attending church with them occasionally—things would be different.

Now there were other things—vague, disturbing things which Rachel hardly dared put into words: Jerry's preoccupation, the late hours he kept, his aura of secretiveness when she questioned him about his activities. He always brushed her off with an excuse that he was working late. Was he? When so many aerospace workers had been laid off for lack of work? But then she reasoned that perhaps Jerry had to assume the duties of those who had been laid off. Certainly it was possible.

But was it the truth? Or could it be that Jerry had found a new interest, *someone else*? Until now she hadn't dared to put the thought into words. Was Jerry involved with another woman? Was their marriage in even deeper trouble than she suspected? Immediately Rachel chastened herself for harboring such suspicions. But the nagging questions could not be erased and Rachel's mind wavered between two poles—the agony that her suspicions might be correct and a gnawing guilt over the fact that she did not trust her husband.

Considering her situation, was it any wonder that Rachel didn't want to face a pregnancy now? How could she afford to bring another life into the tangled web of her marriage? It was all she could do to cope with Jerry and Brian. And lately, if she admitted it, she seemed hardly able to cope with anyone—or anything—at all.

"Mrs. Webber. Mrs. Webber! The doctor will see you now."

Rachel frowned briefly, attempting to swing her thoughts back to the present, trying to recognize the voice that spoke her name. Who called her? But of course—the nurse. Rachel tried to rise casually, but she felt herself on the verge of leaping from her chair. The rotund lady with the gothic novel glanced up momentarily, a flicker of interest lighting behind her eyes. The two teenagers offered curious stares, and Rachel felt an inexplicable impulse to apologize for something, to say, at least, "excuse me."

She said it with her eyes but kept her lips tightly closed as she met the starched woman's professional gaze, then passed through the open door to the examining room.

Twenty minutes later Rachel sat facing Dr. Oberg in his office.

"Ah, yes," the mild-mannered physician hummed brightly. "The lab was prompt with the results." He glanced at the slip of paper he held as if it were a cue card and, with a smile, informed her, "The test was positive, Mrs. Webber."

"Positive?" she echoed. "Are you sure? Couldn't there be a mistake?"

"Oh, no, Mrs. Webber, it's highly unlikely. The test is 95 percent accurate. And my examination confirms it. You are indeed pregnant." He patted her hand gently, almost a fatherly gesture. "Can I answer any questions for you?"

Rachel was silent.

"Well, then," the doctor told her, resuming an air of formality, "if you would just check with my nurse for your next appointment—"

Rachel walked out of the office, dazed, telling herself, *This can't be real.* It must be someone's clever prank, a hoax. Pregnant. How could she tell Jerry? What would she say? *Surprise! We're going to have a baby. Just what we need.*

On the way home it occurred to Rachel that she would not have to tell Jerry anything at all. Not yet. For the present her pregnancy would remain her secret.

Chapter Two

It was late October, cold and storm-cloudy. Jerry Webber gazed for a few moments into the dreariness outside the window, then turned his attention back to the work at hand. He fished through his desk drawer for paper clips, but as usual, couldn't find anything when he wanted it. Rubber bands, pencils and erasers, scratch paper and marking pens. But no paper clips. Impatiently he slammed the desk drawer, saying something unintelligible under his breath.

Jerry Webber was a tall, handsome man with a face his wife considered strong and sensitive. His arms and face were tanned a reddish brown, giving him a rather rugged, weather-beaten, even seafaring appearance. He looked as if he might have posed for one of those ubiquitous TV ads in which a smiling, more-than-handsome young man claims to be one of the Pepsi generation or uses a certain aftershave. People considered Jerry Webber handsome, a man's man and a woman's man. He was pleased, very pleased, that people considered him attractive.

Paperwork was strewn on his desk top like gigantic pieces of confetti, and now a draftsman stood at his desk wanting to know if he had gone over the check prints of the drawing completed last Friday. Which drawing? The top assembly for the anti-ice system, the draftsman reminded. Yeah, it was here—somewhere.

Sure, he had merely set the Wellman test report on top of it. He would check the drawing once more—quickly. The draftsman left abruptly, only slightly mollified.

Jerry scanned the drawing, remembering now that everything was all right. If the draftsman had waited a minute, he could have taken the check print with him. Now Jerry would have to deliver it personally. Irritated, he wrapped the check print around a roll of vellums for the Hiller job. Might as well deliver everything at once.

Casually he aimed his vision at Kit's desk. She was typing something, unaware of his gaze and of the effect she had on him whenever he looked at her. His irritation was gone, dissolved. With drawings in hand he headed for her desk. Paper clips were a good excuse—a reason to interrupt her work, talk to her, watch the lovely things her face did when she smiled.

"Talk a minute?" he asked when she looked up, startled.

She smiled. "Okay, Jerry. Sure."

He lowered his voice a degree and assumed what he considered a tone of stern authority. "As secretary to the engineering department, you are responsible for keeping us supplied with such indispensable items as paper clips, right? Now if you forsake these small—but important—duties, you'll only go on to greater negligence in the future—"

She stifled a laugh. "Are you out again? What do you do? Eat them?"

"Don't get smart, young lady, or I'll find your supply and pilfer the entire stock. Then where will you be?"

"Right here. With you."

He paused, catching the light in her eyes—the blueness of rivers and lakes and spring waters. A blueness he could swim through and drink of and drown in. "With you?" he repeated. "That sounds good to me."

Her cheeks flushed rose and she grinned. She looked impish when she grinned, as if there were many wonderful secrets locked up in her head which she would share only when she chose to, with whom she chose.

"Here are your paper clips," she announced brightly, removing a small cardboard box from her desk. "Are you planning to make me a necklace?"

"Yeah, but not out of paper clips," he grinned, fumbling with the drawings he forgot he was holding. "Say, Kit," he added softly, making his voice sound as if they were still talking about paper clips. "Kit, do you want to get a bite to eat after work?"

Her voice showed surprise. "I thought you had to be home tonight."

"I just phoned Brian a few minutes ago, and he said Rachel is out shopping. He doesn't know when she'll get home. So I told him I have to work late. I thought we'd at least have time to grab a steak sandwich and talk a little. I'm sorry it can't be more—"

"No, that's all right. I'd like to. I'll have to call my roommate. She thought I'd be home—"

"Well, if you'd rather wait until we can go some place nice—"

"No, Jerry, not at all. It's just that she was going to try something fancy for dinner. A souffle or something. She won't want to bother just for herself. I'll let her know so she can put in a TV dinner or something."

"I'm sorry I couldn't let you know sooner."

"That's okay. I'm just glad for the chance to be with you. You know that."

"Yeah, me, too. Meet you in the parking lot, okay?"

"Sure."

Jerry Webber delivered the check print and vellums, then returned to his desk and shuffled idly through the odds and ends of paperwork—government specifications, purchase orders, and engineering estimate forms. He worked mindlessly with the paper clips, attaching them to the corners of papers, but his eyes—and his thoughts—remained on Kit across the room. Finally, at least to appear occupied, he scanned the current issue of *Aviation Week*.

After work, because their time together was so limited, Jerry drove Kit to the Hamburger House, where they took a booth and ordered. This place was perfect, only blocks from Kit's apartment and halfway between work and his home. It was a spot usually crowded at this hour with the after-five teenage traffic from the nearby junior college.

Jerry enjoyed watching the limber bodies of the young, tall as poles, graceful as velvet sashes strung in the breeze. His son Brian was a teenager now. One day a child you could wrestle with and jounce in the air. One day a child, and the next . . . Now Brian was reaching into another world. Perhaps he would be swept up like all the others, forced to join and conform or to test and try the limits. Most likely, he would attempt to defy the established order of things. It was expected now.

Still, it startled Jerry to find himself massing his son with all the others—the rebels, the freaks, even the majority of good kids who only experimented with one thing or another. Morals were like that now. Everyone saw what he wanted to see, even Jerry. He did what he pleased, stretched the limits and rearranged the boundaries. Brian would be no different—no better and no worse.

"Are you coming back soon?"

"What?"

Kit was sitting across from him in the booth, beaming, a peculiar half-smile on her lips. "I said, if you don't come back soon from wherever you have wandered, I'm going to steal your dill pickle and carrot sticks."

"I'm sorry, Kit, I was thinking about Brian. Be my guest to the carrot sticks."

"Is Brian in some kind of trouble?"

"No, not at all. He loves eighth grade. He's doing well, I think. No complaints from anyone, as far as I know."

"Well, then?"

"I was imagining him being like these kids that come in here. They're a whole new breed, you know?"

"And it's hard to picture Brian being one of them, right?"

"I guess so."

"He'll do okay. From what you've told me, he's a great kid."

"He is," Jerry agreed, shaking steak sauce on his sandwich.

"I wish I could meet him."

Jerry glanced up, startled. He felt his neck muscles tighten. "I wish you could too, Kit. But it's just not possible. You know that."

The girl flushed. "Jerry, I'm sorry. I didn't mean anything by that. It was just an idle remark. I'm not trying to push you, Jerry. Really, I'm not."

"I know, Kit. I'm sorry. I get wound up sometimes and shoot off my big mouth."

"But I know I don't make things any easier for you."

"It's not your fault, Kit. It's just the way things are."

"For what it's worth, Jerry, I adapt easily," she said.

"If this is it—what we have now, fine. If more comes, that's fine, too. If not, I understand. Do you know what I'm saying, Jerry?"

"Yeah, I know, Kit. You don't want to push me into a corner. But you know as well as I do that things can't stay as they are. They have to go one way or another. Relationships aren't static; they're alive—"

"I know, Jerry. But like you've said before, we'll take our time."

Jerry reached across the table for her hand. "That won't be easy, Kit," he warned with a smile. "Not for a guy who thinks he's beginning to fall in love."

Chapter Three

The late October sky was rain-swollen and color-streaked. It had not started to storm yet, but it would, and soon. As Rachel aimed her lime-green LTD homeward through late-afternoon traffic, she conceived in her mind how the evening would be. After nearly two weeks of guarded silence, tonight she would tell Jerry about the baby. Before he arrived home, she would cook fresh broccoli, toss a salad, and put in potatoes to bake. Then she would prepare the porterhouse steaks she had just purchased for the broiler. She had forgotten to pick up sour cream, but she could whip up Jerry's favorite cheese sauce, and there were fresh mushrooms in the refrigerator. Perhaps they could even eat by candlelight, or was that considered gauche now? She would decide later.

Once dinner was started, Rachel could change into something else, perhaps one of her long evening things. The orange-flowered silk—Jerry liked that. She would wait until they had eaten—probably wait even until Brian was in bed—before telling him about the baby. She would be calmer; so would he. They would discuss things intelligently. Perhaps it would not really be so bad. Perhaps a baby would not be a catastrophe after all.

Brian was home, sprawled on the sofa, watching the six o'clock pro football game on television. On entering the room, Rachel felt an immediate surge of irritation. Brian's feet were propped on the coffee table, and he was eating potato chips on her good sofa. He looked up and must have sensed her feelings, for he swung his feet to the floor and pushed the bag of chips into a corner of the couch.

She forced the irritation out of her voice when she asked, "Have you been home long, Brian?"

"Yeah, a little while."

"You came right home from school then?"

"Uh-huh."

Rachel set down her purse and removed her coat. "I thought maybe you would be with your friends."

"No." He hesitated. "I was wondering though," he began. "I met this guy at school today, Ronnie Mayhew. He's ahead of me—in the ninth grade. He's a neat guy, Mom, and I wondered if he could come over tonight? He's going to bring some of his cassette tapes."

"You want someone to come over here, Brian?" Rachel's mind was racing. Tonight had to be special, and there was still so much to do. She stalled. "This is a school night, remember?"

"Yeah, but Ronnie's ma said he can come if it's all right with you."

"I don't know—"

"Mom, most of the time ninth graders don't pay much attention to us guys in the lower grades." Her son sat up, leaning forward, his neck and arms angular, his shoulders taut, as if somehow he had to impress upon her physically the importance of his request. She chose to ignore it.

"Brian—Brian, not tonight, please. Maybe tomorrow. Ask him for tomorrow night."

The boy scowled. "Yeah, sure. He probably won't want to come then."

"Then he's not much of a friend."

"Aw, Mom, come off it."

"That's enough, Brian." Rachel wasn't winning this one at all. She didn't want to contend with Brian now when there was so much on her mind, so much to do, to plan. Should she take him into her confidence so that he could be her ally? She looked at him, searching his face, and wondered for a moment just who her son was now.

Last year, when Brian was 12, he seemed small to Rachel; his face was plain and round, unmarked, still sweet, a child's face. His body was still a child's body too, soft and smooth. The bodies of young girls and boys seemed alike, all soft and smooth. They all had untouched faces, open and wide and wondering.

Now Brian was 13, and already his face had begun to close, to change, to take on new facets and meanings somewhere behind the eyes. Now his body was suddenly stretching, breaking through the softness, making angles of his arms and legs. In just one year a shrewdness and a new curiosity had registered on his face, around his mouth.

As if to confirm the unseen changes, Brian's face was no longer smooth. Hints of pimples appeared on his chin and forehead. He was becoming someone Rachel wondered if she knew. It was too soon for this sort of thing, too soon. The changes, coming so fast, left Rachel a little bewildered at times, confused as to how she should handle her son. Should she treat him as a child? As a man? He was Brian, whoever Brian was becoming. But she could not think of Brian now.

She sat down beside her son and put the potato chip

bag on her lap. She rolled the slick edges of the bag between her fingers, unaware she was doing so. "Brian," she said, "I didn't want to go into this until I talked with your father, but I guess there's no reason you can't know now."

"Know what, Mom?" He had slouched back against the cushions, his eyes cool, watching her.

"Do you remember when I went to the doctor's for a check-up a couple weeks ago, Brian? Well, I found out . . . I found out that I'm going to have a baby."

He sat up. The amazement in his voice was genuine. "You're kidding, Mom."

"No, I'm afraid not."

"A baby? That's really something. I mean, I never thought of a baby. You aren't too old or anything? I mean, how come a baby?"

The irritation was returning. "I didn't plan it, Brian, if that's what you mean," she snapped. Then, more softly, "It was a surprise to me too, Brian."

"Does Dad know?" he quizzed eagerly.

Rachel shook her head. "No, I haven't told him yet."

"Boy, will he be flipped out. When are you going to tell him?"

"I'll tell him tonight, after dinner. That's why I'd rather your friend come over another time."

"Yeah, I see. Okay," he said, nodding, then added, "But Dad won't be home for dinner."

"Why not?"

"Well, he called earlier and I told him you were out shopping. He said he had to work late anyway and would get a bite on the way home."

"Great," she sighed. "There go the porterhouse

steaks and candlelight I had planned."

"We still gotta eat, you know."

Rachel felt deflated. Her energy had vanished. "How about a McDonald's hamburger?" she said.

"How about the Hamburger House, where Dad takes us sometimes? They have great malts."

She was too tired to argue. "All right, if you get the food to take out. I don't feel like going in."

Rachel drove Brian to the Hamburger House and waited in the car while he went in for hamburgers, malts, and French fries. She sat with the window rolled partly down, her fingertips lightly tapping the steering wheel, her eyes momentarily catching a glimpse of passing strangers, focusing briefly on a gas station being torn down across the street, moving casually to the neatly-lettered window signs advertising the special of the week: Fudge Sundae Delight, w/whipped cream and nuts, 95¢.

The sky had remained the same. Dusky gray clouds ready to burst into drenching rain hovered overhead, swollen and heavy like a great woman in waiting, like she herself would be in time. Why didn't it just rain and get it over with? Why did things have to stand still, horribly, oppressively still?

Rachel's mind was somewhere else, not connected to her eyes, not really concerned with anything she saw so she might have missed Jerry and the girl entirely. At first she only vaguely realized it was Jerry coming out the door, Jerry and a girl who looked familiar and yet was a stranger.

Rachel's first impulse was to call out to her husband, to say, "Here I am, Jerry. Funny to run into you here." The impulse was squelched immediately by something else, a dread, a terrible disappointment. Jerry was with some girl! Who was she? Why were they together? He was supposed to be at the office, working late.

Could she be wrong? Could it be someone who only looked like Jerry? But no. She watched as they went to a car and got in. It was Jerry's car, his little red Mustang with the Auto Club sticker on the bumper. It was Jerry. The way they had walked, the two of them, the way his hand touched her shoulder and her waist as he helped her into the car suggested there was something between them. Rachel could feel it like a shock. They were more than acquaintances. There was something between them, and the knowledge of it shot through Rachel's body like hot gunfire, leaving her wrists and ankles weak, useless. Her worst suspicions had been confirmed and the plain facts made her numb. Jerry and the girl got into his car and drove away without seeing Rachel there at all.

Chapter Four

"Are you hungry, Jerry?" Rachel asked, watching her husband with cool, careful eyes.

"No," he said. He was loosening his tie, pulling it off from around his neck. "Where's Brian?"

"In his room, studying."

"Is there any beer in the icebox?"

"I don't know. You can check."

"How about you? You check, okay? I'm bushed."

"All right." Rachel went to the kitchen and returned to the living room with an open can of beer. Jerry took it, drank, and set the can on a coaster on the table. He unbuttoned his shirt, found the evening newspaper, the *Press-Telegram*, and sat down in his chair, the one that was adjustable to several positions. He tilted back and opened the paper.

"I heard today the cost of living went up another half a percent last month," he said from behind the paper, his voice sounding as if he weren't really talking to anyone in particular and didn't care whether he got a reply.

"Half a percent," he repeated. "And things so shaky in aerospace. You know, one of these days they're going to have all of us walking the bread line, engineers and all." He didn't bother to identify who "they" were. Instead he took another drink, then set the can back into the coaster. "They laid off three guys last week, three of them, and I mean they weren't janitors or clerks. They were top guys, right up there. I tell you, sometimes I think the bottom is ready to fall out of everything." For a moment, he became absorbed in an item in the paper. When he spoke again, he picked up the same thread of conversation. "I shouldn't gripe, I suppose," he said. "I'm doing all right. No one's taken a hatchet to my job yet."

Sitting silently on the sofa, her legs crossed comfortably, listening to Jerry ramble on amiably, Rachel wondered if her mind might be playing tricks on her. This was just like any other night, like every night. Jerry in his chair, having a beer, reading the paper, talking about work and the economy and what was happening to whom. It was all very natural, very right. Only it wasn't right, not when she forced her mind to remember the afternoon, the crazy mixed-up afternoon.

Surely she hadn't seen Jerry today with another woman, some mysterious girl, someone he seemed to know so well, whom she, Rachel, didn't know at all. Certainly nothing existed except tonight, this moment, everything orderly, quiet, and in its place. Should she shatter this peace? Should she force the issue, the issues—Jerry and the girl, the baby, the whole, vague, uncertain direction of their lives? Was she really up to all that? She could keep her mouth shut and go to bed. Shut up and sleep and sleep and sleep. But then things would be no different tomorrow.

"Jerry," she began tentatively. Her face felt strained, her mouth screwed up too tight to speak. "Jerry," she said again, "how come if things are so bad they have you working overtime so much?"

He sat the paper down and gave her a blank look.

"What do you mean by that?"

I just wondered, that's all."

"I have a lot to do. They give me work the other guys used to do, the guys they laid off."

"I see." Her voice was the size of a pin prick, light, airy.

Jerry gave her a second look, close, scrutinizing. "Is something wrong, Rae?" He called her that sometimes. "Are you all right?"

"Sure. I had a bad day, I guess." Might as well plunge ahead, might as well. "Something funny happened, Jerry," she said. "I can't figure it. I saw you today, Jerry, but you didn't see me."

Jerry's expression stayed the same, his eyes watching her, but something in his face seemed to change, shift. "You did? Where?"

"At the Hamburger House. We—Brian and I—went there for dinner. We took the food out. We came home and ate."

"The Hamburger House?" A light had come on in Jerry's eyes, a cool, dazed brightness, as if his mind were weighing many things at once, so that he could not yet speak. Finally he said, "What were you doing at the Hamburger House?"

Rachel looked at him, surprised. "I just told you. Brian and I—"

"Oh, yes, I know that, but I mean . . . well, why didn't you say something if you saw me?"

"You were busy, Jerry. You were with someone."

As if light had dawned, Jerry broke into an extravagant laugh. "Oh, you mean Kit. You saw me with Kit Cannon." He settled back and picked up his paper again, as if by such a gesture he was dismissing a topic too insignificant to pursue. From behind the paper, his voice flowed evenly, nonchalant. "Kit is the secretary in our department. Her car wasn't running so I gave her a ride home. Neither of us had eaten, and it was getting late, so we picked up a sandwich. You should have called to us, Rachel. You should have said something."

She shrugged uncertainly. "You looked so engrossed, I felt like an outsider. I felt—" Rachel was aware of her voice growing quivery all of a sudden. She thought she might cry. Was it relief? What? "I didn't mean to sound stupid, Jerry, like a suspicious wife or something. It's just that I had a big dinner planned, and then there you were—"

"I called and said I had to work, Baby."

"I know you did. But it seems like you have to work so much lately, and I had this idea about tonight being special." On impulse, Rachel got up and went over to Jerry, slipping onto the arm of his chair, letting her arm circle his shoulder, resting lightly, carefully. "I guess I couldn't stand seeing you look so happy with that girl. I mean, you really looked so happy."

"Rachel, will you stop it! Stop hounding me. I told you what happened. I'm sorry you were upset."

Rachel eased her body off the chair arm, going down on her knees, sitting like a silly, foolish schoolgirl. She was looking at her husband as if she might be begging, as if she might be screaming for something inside, screaming against the complete silence of her mouth, her lips.

Jerry's hand, large and manly, came to rest on Rachel's shoulder, found the back of her neck and rubbed gently, soothingly. "I didn't mean to shout, Rae. Really, I'm sorry. It's just that I don't think you have to go on like this about Kit."

"Are you in love with her?" This a whisper, hardly spoken, this from Rachel who could not believe she had asked it.

The directness of the question took Jerry by surprise. He said, "I don't know."

The two of them had been sitting in a calm, orderly room surrounded by stable, bulky, well-placed furniture, with soft light emanating from quiet lamps and everything proper, in its place, where it belonged. This room, one segment of their apartment, was fine, and she and Jerry had been fine until this moment, having a serious but comprehensible discussion.

Now nothing was right at all, and nothing Rachel could do would make it right. In a moment, less than a moment, neither the room nor Jerry nor Rachel made any sense at all.

It was bizarre, this conversation. It was idiotic, the whole thing. What was she doing asking Jerry about being in love with another woman?

"Well, you asked me," Jerry said defensively, seeing the look on her face. "You asked me, so I figured you knew. You asked if I love her, and I told you the truth. I don't know. You want me to play it straight with you, don't you, Rae?"

"I didn't know anything! I don't know why I said that, why I asked if you love her. I didn't know—" She was confused and could only stammer that she really didn't know anything at all.

He stared at her. "You mean, you really didn't have any idea about Kit? Then why in the world did you bring it up? Why did you have to push me, Rachel? Why couldn't you leave things alone?"

"I don't know—"

"I didn't want to hurt you, Rachel. I could have lied. I started to—! You know I didn't want to hurt you."

"I know," she said, not looking at him, not seeing anything, still dazed, groping with thoughts going on in her own head.

"Blast it all anyway," he said. "This whole world is going to hell, you know that? I'm going to hell, and the whole world, straight to hell. What's the use of anything?"

Hearing this new torment in Jerry's voice, Rachel snapped out of her own preoccupation. Her mind was clearing fast. "Jerry," she said, "let's talk. We have to talk about this. I have to understand what's happening."

"What's the use? I mean, really, what's the use of anything?"

"I have to understand this, Jerry." She felt a sudden urge to reach out and touch him but she held back. Instead, she got up from the floor and went over to the couch and sat down. It was a lovely couch, but there were crumbs from potato chips on it, and she brushed them off. Certainly, she thought, some of these things that had happened could be undone, brushed aside like crumbs, forgotten. She had to find out where she and Jerry stood. "Jerry," she said calmly, "I want you to tell me what's going on."

He had the newspaper in his hands again, rolling it up, twisting and turning it, unaware that he was destroying it with his hands. "I don't know what to say, Rachel," he said, his hands busy with the paper. "What can I say? I mean, Kit and I have gotten to be good friends. We didn't plan anything. We just hit it off, you know. Things sort of clicked. . . ."

"When was this?"

"A couple months ago, I guess. Late in the summer."

"Are you having an affair, Jerry?"

"No. No, Rachel. Believe me, it hasn't gone that far. You might say we're still sort of in the beginning of things, seeing each other now and then, that's all." Suddenly he swore, slamming the paper down on the table, jarring a crystal dish that sat on its polished surface. "I shouldn't be telling you this," he said. "I must be crazy saying anything at all. I must be crazy."

"I want to know, Jerry," said Rachel. "It's only fair—"

Her husband grew suddenly quiet, apparently trying to gather his thoughts. He leaned forward in his chair, his shoulders slumping, round and heavy, his eyes focused somewhere in space. "You know yourself, Rachel," he said, "things haven't been too good between us for quite a long time. You know that."

"We've had problems, yes. . . ."

"Problems? Problems? You bet we've had problems. I'm not excusing myself, believe me, I'm not, but . . . well, I guess it just seemed like an escape to be interested in someone else for a while. It was harmless, Rachel, really."

"But you said—I mean, you don't know if you love this girl, Kit. You said you don't know."

"I don't know."

"But you might . . . you might love her."

"I might love her," he said.

Chapter Five

"Hey, Dad, when did you get home?"

It was Brian, bounding into the room, full of a boy's endless energy, grinning broadly at his dad, his enthusiasm noisy. Lately, it seemed Brian was often this way around his dad, almost joyous, sharing something private, something Rachel couldn't quite touch. But why did he have to come in now? Why now?

"Hi, man," Jerry responded brightly, obviously glad to be off the hook with Rachel for a moment. "I got home a half hour ago. How about you? What's the word?"

"Nothing, Dad. Hitting the books is all. No big deal."

"You'll change your tune one of these days."

"Yeah, yeah, I know. But, hey, how about you? Mom tell you the news?"

Rachel saw Jerry flinch slightly; his smile seeming to freeze on his lips. "What do you mean, Brian? Tell me what?"

"About the baby. You told him, Mom, didn't you?"

"No, Brian." Now Rachel was on the spot. She didn't want it to be like this. "I haven't had a chance. I was going to—"

Jerry pulled himself out of his chair and stood in the middle of the room as if he were not sure what he should do next. "What is this?" he said. "Someone tell me what's going on."

"Brian, go to your room and let me talk to Daddy, would you please?"

"Okay, Mom." He looked at both of them apologetically. "I'm sorry if I spoiled the surprise. I mean, I figured you already told him."

As Brian left the room, Rachel steeled herself for this new encounter. It was her trump card, this baby, but she didn't want to play it now. She didn't want to hold on to Jerry this way, if after all there was anything left of their marriage to hold together.

Jerry stood across from her, his body steeled too, and minced no words. "What is Brian talking about, Rachel? Are you pregnant?"

"Yes."

"In the name of heaven, why didn't you tell me? What kind of game are you playing?"

"You're a good one to talk about playing games," she countered, wishing immediately that she had not spoken.

"Oh, we're back to that, are we?" He made a helpless gesture with his hands and sat down. "Rachel," he said, "don't you understand that whatever happened before tonight isn't important? We have to go on from here, from this moment. We've got to pull things together, you and I. Especially now."

"You mean for the baby."

"Yes, I mean for the baby. For Brian too. For all of us."

It was not in Rachel now to respond coolly, to debate and discuss their lives with objectivity, and she resented Jerry's attempt to settle their lives by logic.

Didn't he understand, couldn't he see, that she was coming apart inside? He wanted to talk about tangible things, about plans, about doing this or that. Rachel was concerned with only one intangible, terribly important fact: Jerry evidently no longer loved her, and he might love—actually might love—somebody else.

"Are you listening to me, Rachel? Didn't you hear anything I said?"

"Yes, Jerry, I heard you, but it's too late!" Didn't everything inside her tell her it was too late? All the terrible particles of herself coming apart—the torn bits and pieces of her logical mind, whatever that was, if she ever possessed such a thing. Everything inside her was ready to revolt, and she thought she might vomit. She stood up as if to head for the bathroom.

"Are you all right?" Jerry asked. "Are you sick, Rachel?"

"I don't know—no, I'm all right. I'm a little dizzy, that's all."

"You should go to bed. Rae, let me help you—" Jerry made a gesture toward her, which she rejected as quickly as it was made. He withdrew, letting her pass by him.

"I'm all right," she said, waving her hand, dismissing him. "I have to be alone, Jerry. I've got to think. I just can't think tonight."

"I'm sorry, Rachel. I really am. I'm sorry for this whole mess."

She turned and stared at him. The urge to cry was on her again, washing over her like warm water, like wonderfully warm rivers that might drown her. But she held back the tears, the desire to let herself weep in Jerry's arms. Instead, she asked, "What about her—this girl?"

"I'll break it off, of course. I won't see her again," Jerry answered matter-of-factly.

"But your feelings. You don't know how you feel—"

"Forget it, Rachel, please. I'll work it out. It'll be okay."

She didn't want to hear this. It wasn't the answer she needed. "Don't bother, Jerry," Rachel said, her voice suddenly high and strangled. "Don't bother with charity. I don't want any of it. I just want you out of here. Get out of here—please!" Now she was truly crying, holding the sobs inside herself.

Jerry's face had turned cold, his expression dazed. He was shaken. "All right, Rachel," he said, already moving stiffly, mechanically, toward their room. "Let me get a few things—I'll need a few things. Let me pack a bag, and I'll get out. I'll get out, if that's what you want."

"Yes," she said, turning away, going to the window.

It was raining finally. The rain poured down and hit the window outrageously, like torrents of tears, like the sudden angry tears in her own eyes.

Chapter Six

Three days after Jerry had gone striding out of their apartment, suitcase in hand and jaw set, Rachel broke out of her self-imposed mourning. It was a sunny day, and she needed to get out.

Not that she could escape her confused feelings—the scorching recriminations, the self-pity, blaming herself one moment for her impulsiveness, resenting Jerry the next for actually walking out at her insistence. As if that's what she wanted, his going. Was it? Who knew? All she knew at the moment, on this sunny and warm day in early November was that she had to get out of herself, out of the house, away. So she and Marlene drove to Laguna Beach to spend the day.

Laguna was one of their favorite places. Somehow the endless clusters of quaint, colorful buildings perched on the hillsides and the little network of streets had managed to escape that steely, glazed look that had become the characteristic of so much of Southern California. Rachel was tired of the endless stark, cold ribbons of freeway twisting and turning, jutting in and out, stripping the landscape of any natural grace.

Laguna Beach was different. The buildings were clever and original. They looked as if they had a history to them, as if many people had given parts of their personalities to these structures. The colorful little shops were crowded with artists' paintings—lovely seascapes, beautiful landscapes, portraits and still lifes.

Many artists came here, hoping to sell their work—the trained and untrained alike. Rachel adored their paintings—the meticulous portraits of old men from the sea, children in soft airy dresses, and the tiny finely crafted canvases of fruit—a single apple or a pear, stark against an ebony background.

Throughout the afternoon, Rachel felt certain that Marlene was bursting with unasked questions. Marlene said nothing but cast frequent sidelong glances at Rachel, no doubt to determine the state of her emotions. Marlene was too polite to bombard her with probing queries about Jerry's sudden move out of the apartment. On the phone the morning after Jerry left, Rachel had spilled out the story in brief choked snatches, leaving it to Marlene to fill in the blanks.

"He's gone and that's all there is to it, Marlene," Rachel had told her friend that morning. "And I just don't want to talk about it anymore; I just can't."

So that was it. Rachel had said no more.

But now Rachel felt better. Relaxed by the pleasant day at Laguna and with her emotions lulled by sea breezes, she felt capable of discussing with some degree of objectivity her present circumstances. She told Marlene everything that came to her mind as they drove home that evening, finishing with: "Yesterday I called a lawyer over in North Long Beach. I had a long talk with him and he said I could come in for an appointment."

"Are you going?"

"I don't know. I'm thinking about it."

"Does that mean you're thinking about getting a divorce?"

"Well, I have to consider it. The thing is, I didn't

46

have any idea how things are now—with the divorce laws and all. The lawyer told me that the California laws were changed drastically a few years ago. It's not a divorce anymore; it's a *dissolution*. All you have to say is that you have irreconcilable differences, and that's it, you can have your divorce. It's just about that easy. Only you have to wait six months, for what he called the interlocutory period, then the whole thing is done with. What do you think of that?"

"It sounds ghastly to me," said Marlene, feigning a shudder. She was driving, and they were on the freeway now, in the fast lane, going 55. Marlene liked to drive and could handle a car as well as anyone. She could drive anywhere, for hours at a time, and not get tired or nervous. When she and Rachel went anywhere, Rachel always let her drive.

"The whole thing sounds awful to me, too," Rachel admitted with a flat little smile. "While I was talking to the lawyer, his voice was so smooth and silky and unconcerned, I thought I must be out of my mind. Here I was talking about Jerry and myself with some stranger like it was nothing at all.

"Anyhow, he said the laws had been changed so that there would be less recrimination and guilt; he kept using those words, recrimination and guilt. There's no blaming anyone now, he said, and he claimed that makes it all a lot easier."

Rachel paused and sighed audibly. The sigh seemed to go all the way through her, somehow snatching her strength, leaving her tired. "There's nothing easy about tearing up a whole part of your life and throwing it away," she said. "He made it sound as easy as wrapping up the garbage and taking it out."

"I just hope you don't go and do anything on impulse, Rachel," warned Marlene.

"Well, the lawyer said you have to pay at least half the fee as soon as you start divorce proceedings. I guess a lot of people get halfway through and change their minds, so the lawyer would be out a lot, I suppose, if he didn't have you pay at the start. Anyway, I don't want to do anything until I'm absolutely sure."

"I was just wondering—have you prayed about all this, Rachel?"

"Well, everything happened so fast I haven't had much chance to pray," Rachel admitted lamely. She did not want to confess that at the moment the thought of praying left her with a terrified, strangled sensation. "I won't do anything without praying about it first," she said, her voice rising a little, "so don't you worry about that."

"It's just that—well, I have this feeling about you, Rachel."

"What? What feeling?"

"I don't know. You're putting me on the spot—I can't explain it."

They were on the off-ramp now, heading for home. The traffic was starting to thicken; it was after 4 p.m. Rachel heard a car horn honking, but it was back on the freeway somewhere. At the end of the off-ramp they had to wait for a signal, one of those endless lights. Rachel switched on the radio and turned the dial, catching snatches of music, most of it rock and roll. One station was playing "Younger than Springtime." She left it on.

"Almost home," said Marlene, a surface brightness to her voice. Then, softly, she asked, "How's Brian taking all of this?"

48

The inquiry hit a vulnerable area. Rachel winced in spite of herself. "I'm afraid Brian's awfully upset," she answered, turning down the radio a bit. "He doesn't say much, but I know he doesn't understand what's happening. He never used to be close to his dad, really, but lately they were hitting it off well together. I have this feeling, Marlene, that Brian resents me now—maybe Jerry and me both. I don't know."

"It's bound to be hard on him, Rachel."

"Well, what about me?" Rachel cried. It was as if a great torrent of anger had suddenly burst upon her, spillings its juices over all the sane and proper emotions she thought were expected of her.

"What about me anyway?" she repeated, her voice shrill. "I have prayed for years, Marlene, you know that. For years I've prayed that Jerry would be saved and that we'd finally have some unity in our family. For years I've gone to church alone and tried to bring up Brian in the church—in spite of his father's influence. Do you think Jerry has ever for one moment bent my way? I kept on and took it all—the loneliness and the lack of communication—because I thought someday Jerry would be saved and things would be different. But now, now he's going with some girl—maybe he's in love with her, I don't know. So what's left, Marlene? What's left of anything?"

"You said Jerry wants to try again—"

"Oh, I know," said Rachel, raking her fingers through her hair, pushing strands of hair off her forehead. There was an expression of futility on her lips and around her eyes that made her face seem slightly distorted. "I know Jerry said that, but I can't see what good it would do. What's going to make things any better?"

"Doesn't it say in the Bible that if a woman has an unsaved husband and he wishes to stay with her, then she shouldn't make him go?" asked Marlene evenly. "Doesn't it say she should stay with him, Rachel?"

"I never read that," Rachel replied, frowning. "I never saw that verse anywhere as far as I can remember." She snapped off the radio with a decisive flick of the wrist, having no desire at all to hear the final verse of "Younger than Springtime."

Chapter Seven

"That's about it," Jerry said with a tone of finality. "That's how things stand between Rachel and me right now. Not too pretty, huh?"

Kit sat beside him in his little red Mustang, her fingers playing with the strap of her purse. He watched her, pleased with her smooth, polished attractiveness, aware of a certain subtle aura of worldliness about her, although she was only 23. It was as if she had learned and accepted all the ways of the world without a second thought. Kit was smaller and darker than Rachel and wore more makeup (always a glossy, magazine sort of look to her face), but if Jerry thought about it at all, Kit was probably no prettier than Rachel, who somehow managed to appear both natural and elegant at once.

Jerry checked his thoughts shortly, alarmed to find himself making such comparisons. He looked more closely at Kit. Her expression was clouded; Jerry couldn't read it. He wondered what she was thinking now that she knew the whole story.

"I'm sorry, Jerry," she said at last. "I'm really sorry."

He had driven her up to Signal Hill to talk. It was one of the few places in Long Beach where there was still a semblance of privacy. The hill was a jutting protuberance of land laced with narrow, weaving roads, its landscape blemished by oil pumps and drilling rigs. The hill was considered by some to be a lovers' lane, and no doubt police cars patrolled the area periodically to encourage reluctant drivers onto the road again.

Jerry wasn't bothered by the hill's reputation, because here he could look out and see the dazzling lights of the Los Angeles basin spread out before him. For Jerry, there was no real darkness in this place where all cities joined together to create one huge metropolis. In this place, this city of cities, there were only lights, like stars.

"I didn't tell you all of this for you to be sorry, Kit," he said, swinging his thoughts back to their conversation. He watched her face, noticing how it was cut into halves by shadow and moonlight. *Moony*, he thought. *She looks wonderfully moony, whatever that might be.* The word stuck in his imagination and seemed to describe her somehow. He squeezed her shoulder affectionately. "Listen, girl," he said gently, "I'm not trying to cry on your shoulder. I just want to be straight with you and let you know how things are with me."

"I understand, Jerry, really I do."

"Good."

"Jerry, just one thing. I wonder—"

"Yeah?"

"Well, Rachel and the baby and all this—how does it . . . how is it going to affect us?"

"What do you mean?"

"I guess I mean, where do we go from here?"

"I don't know," he said, shrugging slightly. "I can't just walk away from Rachel. Especially now, with the baby—"

"I know. But—what can you do?"

He shrugged again, feeling suddenly tired and used

up. He wished he could be asleep, dreaming of something that mattered to no one. "I didn't want to tell Rachel about you, about us, but when it came right down to it, I was glad she knew," he said seriously. "This secrecy and deceit was a monster on my back. I'm glad she knows." He looked at her to see if she agreed, and she nodded solemnly. "The thing is," he continued, "I'm not one of these types of guys who tries to pull off some shady intrigue. Rachel knows that. All I want is a decent life that makes some sense."

"Can you have that with Rachel?"

Jerry looked at her quickly and noted that there was really no malice in Kit's voice. He was glad of that.

"I don't know if I could have that with Rachel or not," he answered. "Doesn't look like I'll get a chance to find out, does it?"

He drove her home and waited patiently, amused while she fished through her purse for her key. Kit carried a large purse and always had to fish for anything she wanted—a Kleenex, her compact, a dollar, whatever.

She found the key and looked up, smiling. "Can you come in a minute?" she asked him. When he didn't answer, she said, "I could fix you some coffee or a sandwich—I have tuna fish or left-over ham. How about it?"

"Not tonight, Kit," he answered. "Your roommate probably needs her beauty sleep, and she'd have our heads if we woke her."

Kit flashed another kind of smile now and said, slyly, "My roommate is in San Diego visiting friends, Jerry. She won't be home until tomorrow afternoon. There's no one to bother us."

Jerry sized up the situation instantly and slowly

shook his head. "No, Kit," he said, "I told Rachel you and I are not having an affair. I was glad I could tell her that." He touched her cheek with his fingertips. "Honey, this whole thing—what we have—could have started out as an affair, and it would probably be over by now—something already forgotten. But that's not what I'm looking for. I don't want more confusion in my life; I want some answers, something with some meaning. I think you and I could find that meaning. I think we could have something of real value, but not if we go too fast. I can't ask anything of you until I can make a commitment, until I know which way my life is going."

"What you don't understand," she said, smiling, pressing his hand against her lips, "is that a commitment isn't necessary. I'm not asking for any commitments, Jerry."

Gently, he retrieved his hand so that he could open the car door. "Perhaps not, Kit," he said soberly, "but I am."

Chapter Eight

In the weeks following her separation from her husband, Rachel found herself thinking frequently of the day she spent with Marlene at Laguna Beach. Out of the wearisome accumulation of days since Jerry left, that day at Laguna stood alone as a sign that life could still be pleasant. She had to hold on to that idea—that life without Jerry could be bearable.

Surprisingly Rachel found herself thinking more and more in terms of *I* instead of *we*. *I* should take the car in for a tune-up. *I* must remember to send Jerry's mother a birthday card. *I* must talk to Brian about his history grade.

She was a woman alone now and would have to assume the responsibilities of a woman alone. There was so much talk these days of what it meant to be a woman, of how she ought to fulfill herself as an individual. During her marriage, Rachel had not taken seriously the arguments and demands of the outspoken advocates of the Women's Liberation Movement. After all, Rachel had known what her obligations were to Jerry and Brian. There had seemed to be no necessity to question her role as wife and mother.

But what was her role now? What were her responsibilities? Jerry was gone. Brian was growing up. Perhaps the time had come for Rachel to look after herself, to consider her own wishes first for a change.

Rachel began to browse with greater interest through the women's magazines at the supermarkets and drugstores. Every magazine seemed to contain articles proclaiming the rights of women. A woman's right to a career. Her right to divorce. Her right to have an abortion.

Her right to an abortion? This idea was especially foreign to Rachel. She was aware that the laws had been liberalized. The Supreme Court had declared that almost any woman could have an abortion if she chose. Abortion on demand, they called it.

But Rachel had not seriously thought about abortion before, not personally. Not in the intimate way that a woman actually considers ending her unborn child's life.

Rachel had always considered abortion wrong, a sin, even murder. Wouldn't it be murder in the eyes of God? Her pastor believed so. But, of course, lately Rachel had not attended church as regularly as before. She did not think about what her pastor might have to say. The truth was that Rachel didn't think about God a great deal now. It seemed that her prayers were becoming vain repetitions, hardly profitable. She was a Christian, but for the present she wasn't giving much thought to what that meant.

So Rachel's mind was open to new ideas and new possibilities. She read avidly, absorbing everything, tasting new concepts as if they were delicacies. Did a woman really have a variety of life-styles to choose from? Did she have the right to control her own body, even to the extent of taking her unborn child's life? Could Rachel actually consider having an abortion?

On one hand it seemed unthinkable. How could any

woman destroy her own helpless baby? On the other hand, Rachel dreaded the thought of raising a child alone. What kind of life could she give a child now? He would be virtually fatherless. Faced with the necessity to work, she would have little time to devote to an infant. Was it possible that the kinder act would be to end the child's life before it began? It seemed lately that women everywhere were answering yes! But how could Rachel voice her secret misgivings—and to whom?

One afternoon Rachel dared to approach Marlene with her question about whether abortion was actually a choice open to her. She drew her words carefully, anticipating what Marlene's reply would be. But she hardly imagined the impassioned response her question would provoke.

"Abortion?" Marlene echoed in stunned disbelief. "Rachel, honey, are you considering an abortion? Listen to me, don't you even think of such a thing. Not ever, do you hear? You better go home and get yourself straightened out with God!"

Duly chagrined, Rachel slumped home, her questions unanswered and her intentions unresolved. The agony of indecision tore at her mind.

Rachel realized that she should have known better than to reveal her inner thoughts about an abortion to Marlene. Marlene saw everything in terms of black and white, and, what's more, she seemed to have no trouble determining what was black and what was white. If only I could see things with equal clarity, Rachel lamented.

When Jerry stopped by to pick up Brian for a ball game one Saturday afternoon, Rachel again— inadvertently—stumbled on to the subject of abortion. Jerry had asked how she was feeling and made some comment about the baby's birth. When Rachel appeared hesitant, Jerry pressed her for information.

"Is something wrong? Is there some problem with your pregnancy?"

Rachel shook her head, flustered, groping for words. "No, everything is all right. But I—I don't know if I want to have the baby."

Jerry stared incredulously at her. "What are you saying? Are you saying—"

The words escaped in a whisper. "I'm thinking about an abortion."

"An abortion!" he exploded.

"It's legal now, you know," she said defensively. "Women do it all the time."

"But not you, Rachel. I know you too well."

Rachel felt herself wavering. "I don't know what I'm going to do."

"It's my baby too, you know," Jerry argued.

Before she could answer, Brian came into the room, greeting his father with a loud, "Hey, Dad, you're here! I'm just about ready." Meanwhile, Rachel escaped to the kitchen.

What are the powers of a woman? What are her rights? What are the responsibilities of a Christian woman? Rachel weighed these questions over and over, until her head throbbed. The more she sought an answer, the more clouded her thoughts became. Finally, in desperation, she called her doctor and asked for the number of a social agency offering counseling on abortion. With hands trembling, she called the agency and made an appointment.

It was done simply enough. The following afternoon Rachel sat primly in a neat, modern outer office where two other women sat waiting. One of the women, no more than a teenager, browsed nervously through a fashion magazine. The middle-aged woman beside her sat stiffly, her lips drawn in a severe line, her eyes focused on the opposite wall.

No doubt they were a trapped, frightened daughter and an injured, indignant mother, Rachel surmised.

When at last it was Rachel's turn to sit down in the private office of Mrs. Olive Kent, counselor, Rachel had an impulse to turn and run the other way. She quelled the impulse and folded her cold, clammy hands in her lap while Mrs. Kent jotted something on a sheet of paper. After a moment, the woman looked up at Rachel and smiled pleasantly.

"You are Rachel Webber. Is that *Miss* or *Mrs.*?"

"Mrs.," Rachel replied. "But we're separated."

"I see," murmured Mrs. Kent thoughtfully, writing again. She turned her eyes back to Rachel, lightly touching the tip of her pen to her lower lip as she spoke. "Now how long have you been pregnant, Mrs. Webber?"

"Two—well, almost three months now."

"And you are considering an abortion."

Rachel opened her mouth to speak. A dry throat cut off her words. A phrase was pounding over and over in her mind, "Wait on the Lord; be of good courage." What that had to do with abortion, Rachel had no idea, but the phrase stayed with her anyhow.

"You are considering abortion?" repeated Mrs. Kent patiently.

"I don't know what I'm doing here," whispered Rachel.

"I'm sorry," began Mrs. Kent uncomprehendingly.

"What did you say?"

"I don't belong here," said Rachel urgently. She gathered her coat and purse and stood up. Mrs. Kent watched in perplexed silence as Rachel excused herself and hurried out of the office.

Driving home, Rachel whispered again and again, "God forgive me for trying to take it out of Your hands."

That same afternoon Rachel telephoned Jerry and told him there would be no abortion. Her mind was clear. Whatever happened, their baby had a right to live..

Chapter Nine

Brian Webber had four days off from school for the Thanksgiving holidays. Four whole days! Two days were the regular weekend he'd have anyway, but the four days together made more than half a week. You could do a lot of things with more than half a week.

Brian was 13. The first three months of eighth grade were behind him. It was no big thing anymore being in eighth grade. He was settled into the dreary routine of homeroom and classes and cafeteria lunches and more classes and only now and then a school assembly to break the monotony of it all. He was looking forward to ninth grade, which was really the first year of high school. Reaching a goal like that might make the tedium bearable. Being in high school was a lot better than saying, "I'm in the eighth grade."

Brian's friend, Ronnie Mayhew, was in the ninth grade, and he let you know it. He waved it around like a flag, his being a *freshman*. Actually, Ronnie was 15 and should have been in tenth grade, but he had flunked a grade somewhere back in elementary school. He didn't like to say much about it, and Brian, being respectful, never brought the subject up.

This past year had been a mystery to Brian. Until this year he had not thought particularly about who he was or what he was doing. Certain things were expected of him and he did them. He had never had to weigh his actions against other possible actions. He did what he was told by his parents, his teachers and the Sunday school teachers. He was a good boy, everyone said. Not until this year had he considered that he might not be a good boy, that there might be other choices open to him.

It was an electrifying thought to a vulnerable, questioning 13-year-old. When he thought about the choices opening up to him he felt giddy inside, possessed of some magical power—the ability to choose for himself. He kept these thoughts private, churning them over and over in his mind, savoring them like pieces of candy.

However, such delicious thoughts of power and choice always managed to melt away as Brian was pulled back into the routine of the day, the regimen of history lessons, English assignments, book reports and outside reading. He was involved also in track, and there was the photography club after school on Tuesday nights.

And there were his church obligations: he was chairman of his Sunday school class, although he had never been certain just what the title implied or what was expected of him in that position. He was also on the social committee for his Sunday evening youth group. Those duties were usually pleasant, involving the planning of special Friday night activities—bowling, pizza parties, cook-outs, or scavenger hunts. He got a kick out of arranging things; he liked taking charge. "Have Brian do it. He'll take care of everything," the other kids would say. He liked that.

Brian considered himself a Christian. He had no doubt about certain things. Jesus, for one. Jesus was in him, and Jesus was God Himself. There were times when Brian could almost feel the power of Jesus welling up inside him, and he felt nothing was impossible for him with Jesus as his best friend. Yes, the two of them together were an unbeatable combination.

At other times, however, things got blurry and out of focus, and Brian's ideas of Jesus got mixed up with his image of Mr. Lipton, his Sunday school teacher, a timorous little man who wore baggy trousers and rarely understood the language of eighth graders. Brian felt sorry for Mr. Lipton and would always dutifully sit still during his lessons, perhaps to make up for the restlessness, the whispers, and shuffling of feet of the other guys in the class. But Brian also resented having to sit so still when he was anxious to get up and go do something. He wished Mr. Lipton would wise up and quit teaching Sunday school and go take up the collection or something.

Once Brian had had a really good Sunday school teacher, Ray Johnson, who was 23 and played football in college. Mr. Ray, as they called him, always had something to say that made his students think. Brian learned that it was fun to think past the surface grooves that everybody usually fell into.

It was Mr. Ray who led Brian to the Lord and Mr. Ray who got him to pray out loud in class and memorize Scripture. But then last year Ray Johnson had married and taken a job in Cleveland, Ohio, so now probably another bunch of kids somewhere in Cleveland were getting the benefit of Ray Johnson.

Thinking about it now, it seemed to Brian that it had been years since Ray Johnson was part of his life. Maybe it was because so many of Brian's feelings and attitudes had changed this past year. He was back to that. Back to this new confusion, this new ecstasy of choices. Who did he really have to be responsible to? Himself? He hardly knew yet what he wanted from himself. Responsible to his parents? Them?

Who were they anymore? Who? They didn't even live together now. They were *separated*. Maybe they would get a divorce. Brian knew other kids who had divorced parents. He thought there was always sort of a strangled, befuddled look about them, these kids with divorced parents—as if they were being secretly pulled in several directions at once and had no idea in the world how they had gotten into such a predicament.

Brian did not want to be like those kids. He pitied them, because they were helpless to change anything. There was no way they could pull things together, and Brian hated to think that anyone should have to be so helpless. It wasn't fair, and Brian wanted no part of anything unfair.

But now, whether he liked it or not, Brian was like those other kids, helpless and open-eyed with puzzlement. He hated it.

Brian was certain he loved his parents, both of them, in different ways. But he also hated them, although this was a sin. He hated them most of all the night his dad left. Why did he leave all of a sudden, without warning, with no hint at all to prepare Brian for this sudden hurt? And what about his mother, who loved Jesus just as Brian did—why hadn't she loved his father enough to stop him? Brian was convinced that adults were strange people who rarely did things the way one would expect. They demanded so much more from things, from people, so that life was always more complicated than it appeared on the surface.

Brian simply could not help feeling confused about his parents, about his own affections and loyalties. It seemed to him that most of his life he had been closer to his mother than to his father, for it was he and his mother who went together to church each week and who prayed together at night. He was just a small boy, eight years old, when these patterns were established, but even then, he sensed that he was right to go his mother's way.

His father was a strong handsome man who kept all things to himself, who said little or nothing, and because Brian did not really know his father, he feared him a little. His father never went with them to church, and religion was not discussed in his presence. God belonged to Brian and his mother, and to bring God before his father would have been awkward for all of them. There were a few occasions Brian could remember when his father had dressed up in one of his really sharp suits and had gone with them to church—to a Christmas play or the Bible school children's program or an Easter cantata. Brian was always overwhelmingly proud of his father during these occasions. After all, some of the church kids doubted that Brian even had a father. "You mean, you have a father? I never saw him, not in two years," someone said to him once. Brian never forgot.

"I have a handsome, successful father," he wanted the world to know. And now that he was getting older, Brian felt that he understood his father better—and perhaps envied him a little, his power to do what he pleased. Perhaps that was why Brian felt a new sort of camaraderie between his father and himself. They were men and shared a man's power and love of freedom. It was a mystery, this power of men, that Brian was anxious to unravel and claim for himself.

Someday Brian would be free to come and go like his father. He would be his own boss. He would have a man's freedom.

Over the years Brian had wondered what his father did during those free hours while his wife and son were at church. What did he do with so much free time and all the rooms of the house to himself? Brian knew his dad slept late on Sunday mornings, and sometimes when they got home at noon, his father was still sitting at the breakfast table drinking a cup of black coffee, reading the Sunday paper. Brian wondered what this private world of his dad's was like—that he had to answer to no one, not to Brian, not to Rachel, apparently not even to God.

Brian's mother was easier to understand and perhaps not so interesting as his father. She had always put God and the church first, and then Brian and Brian's father before herself. It was that simple. Brian felt that he could always count on her to do whatever was *right*. Right was a mystical word to his mother. Right had priority over everything else, even over a person's own desire for something. There were times when Brian wished he could tell his mother to do what *she* wanted to do for a change—it would have been better, he thought, than having her do something only because it was the "right" thing to do. But these instances were vague in his mind, and if he was aware that at times his mother was resentful of something, it was not a reality he could grasp or cope with. So he left it alone.

Actually, if he thought about it, he could not be sure how his mother felt about things now. So much had happened lately. It only confused Brian to try to guess what was going on in the minds of either of his parents anymore. In fact, it seemed to Brian that the time had come when his parents were no longer his primary interest. He figured that part of it no doubt was that he was growing up. And, of course, now that his parents seemed to be flying off crazily in opposite directions, he could not think of them without feeling a little sick inside.

Now, at the age of 13, it seemed terribly important to Brian to win the respect and admiration of someone like Ronnie Mayhew, a ninth grader, who was already 15 and wise to the world. There was a quality of intoxication about Ronnie, a swaggering sort of confidence that held Brian spellbound. He was hypnotized by Ronnie's worldliness, by his apparent ability to cope with anything that was thrown at him. In contrast, Brian felt within himself a terrible vulnerability to life, a quality he tried feverishly to hide from every living soul. No one must know that he was unsure of himself, that he could be hurt by people. So, if it had been possible, Brian happily would have absorbed all of the boldness and self-confidence Ronnie possessed.

The next best thing was for Brian to hang around Ronnie long enough so that this aura of self-confidence would rub off on him. It was for this reason primarily that Brian chose Ronnie Mayhew to be his best friend.

Chapter Ten

Ronnie Mayhew, a tanned, swaggering, blunt-nosed kid in too-tight faded jeans, was barely passing in school. He let it be known to anyone who listened that as soon as he turned 16 he was going to get out of that lousy school and get himself a job where he could make some money—real money. Ronnie Mayhew smoked pot and it was rumored around that he turned on little kids, fifth and sixth graders. No one knew for sure, but that's what was said.

Ronnie never brought up the subject with Brian, and Brian had no desire to discuss it either, since dope was one of the really terrible sins, terribly dangerous, and better left alone. The very thought of it frightened Brian.

While Ronnie did not mention drugs to Brian, he did bring up the subject of shoplifting, describing it as one of his more entertaining pastimes. A guy who was really with it could shoplift and never be caught, he said. A guy who lost his cool—or who wasn't willing to try in the first place—was a mama's brat, a real loser, a first-class jerk.

Ronnie fascinated Brian with his tales of going into department stores and lifting cameras, cassette tape recorders, even stereo record albums, right in front of smart-mouthed clerks who never saw a thing. He was sly, Ronnie was. Brian had no idea how much was truth and how much was fiction. It hardly mattered as long as

Ronnie boasted so convincingly of his escapades. To Brian's mind, it took courage just to speak of such things.

There was none of this reckless courage within Brian; there was only a hopeless sort of longing to be considered Ronnie's equal. Listening to Ronnie, living vicariously through Ronnie's experiences, Brian inevitably came up short by comparison. It was a real pity that he could think of nothing significant about himself, about Brian Webber. What could he do? How could he ever come to possess the guts of a Ronnie Mayhew?

It was with these thoughts in mind coupled with immense self-doubt that Brian Webber executed his first attempt at shoplifting. After giving the matter a great deal of thought, he chose the Friday following Thanksgiving as the day to prove himself. On Thanksgiving Eve, lying on his back on his neatly-made bed, his hands cupped under his head, Brian deliberated a great while over what type of store he ought to select—grocery, department store, five-and-dime, drugstore? Large or small? How did one go about determining such a thing? How could he decide? Finally, swinging his legs over the side of the bed, he resolved that a local discount store would be his first target.

On Thanksgiving Day, alone with his mother, Brian was silent, locked into his secret thoughts. His emotions swung back and forth like a pendulum, so that he was at first enthralled and then appalled by the prospects of the coming day.

Throughout the day, Brian wondered periodically if it was really in him to break the law, to commit such a crime, a sin. Would Jesus forgive him? Would He? But Brian could hardly ask forgiveness yet—when he had not even done the evil deed. Would God forgive him later? He considered praying, but Ronnie Mayhew was closer to him now than God. He even thought of talking to his parents, but who were they now—and where were they really? They were at separate poles, each flying out forever into some mystical region beyond him. They would never come back (though his mother was with him every day and he saw his father on weekends). They were gone, both of them, inexplicably, eternally gone.

In a calm, perfunctory fashion, Brian dressed and ate his breakfast on Friday morning. He said goodbye to his mother, putting his lips to her smooth cheek, and got on his bike and rode away into the cool, smudged California sunlight. He parked his bike in the rack on the sidewalk several yards from the discount store, his chosen victim.

He went into the store in smooth, even strides, his shoulders square, his eyes straight ahead, unblinking. He was a boy with a purpose.

Inside the store, there was the hustle of people with shopping carts and packages and small children, the low hum of voices, the scuffle of feet, the indefinite odor in the air of vegetables and fruits, and the faint smell of freshly-cut beef from behind the meat counter. Brian passed through the grocery area and headed for housewares. His eyes roved critically over the dishes, the pots and pans, the utensils and towels and assortments of things women found ways of using in their kitchens: There was nothing here.

In addition to the usual hum of activity within the store, Brian was aware of another hum, high-pitched and intense, in his own head. It seemed to increase as he padded in his tennis shoes down one aisle and up another. He sauntered over to the record department and stopped to read the list of the top ten on the charts. He browsed through some of the higher-priced record albums—there was no way he could take a record. He had made a hole in his jacket pocket so that when he took something it would drop through the hole into the lining of his coat. He could hold several small items that way—a jack knife, a fountain pen, a cassette tape perhaps—any number of small useful items, but a record album was out of the question. Besides, he had to be careful. Very careful.

Take your time, take it easy, he told himself, forcing his thoughts against the incessant hum in his head. The hum was becoming a pressure. What was he doing? Was he going crazy, walking around looking for something to steal? He examined a small leather case that contained nail clippers, a file, and other gadgets that were attached to a red velvet insert within the case. His dad could use something like that. He turned it over in his hand, feeling the leather. The price tag said $4.95.

"May I help you, young man?" asked the clerk, a pale little man in a gray suit, a bright red tie his only distinguishing feature. The tie overpowered him, even Brian could see that. The little man was all red tie.

"No, sir," Brian said, releasing the leather case as if it had caught fire. "I'm just looking, just looking, sir."

Brian walked away, forcing himself to pace his steps. Don't look like you're running; don't look suspicious, you big dope!

He was getting nervous. He would have to do something fast. It was now or never—do it or forget it. He returned to the record department where they kept cassette tapes. Some places locked up their prerecorded tapes so that kids couldn't get at them. But here they were out in the open on a cardboard display on the counter. Brian read the titles on the tapes, wondering which one he should take. Elvis? The Carpenters? The pressure in his skull was increasing. He could imagine two strong hands squeezing the soft jelly-substance of his brain, crushing his thoughts and plans, twisting his reason. What was the matter with him? What kind of dumb, scared chicken was he anyway?

He selected a tape—"Folsom Prison Blues," by Johnny Cash, attempted to slam the plastic cartridge into his jacket pocket, fumbled with the opening of the pocket and missed the mark. The tape careened to the tile floor, making a sharp "thwack" sound as it hit the floor. Embarrassed, flustered, Brian knelt to retrieve the item, bringing it swiftly back to its place on the counter.

He looked up into the face of a clerk—a thick, stern-faced woman with flaring nostrils—who stared back at him from behind dark-rimmed, suspicious spectacles. She knew—guessed—everything! Brian was sure of it—just as he was sure that at that very moment he might strangle and die at her feet.

"You want to buy it?" she said.

Brian's body was withering, shriveling up, under the woman's critical gaze. She remained imperturbable, watching him. Brian turned on his heel and directly left the store. No looking back, not once. Straight out, man, away! He hopped on his bike and pedaled swiftly home, breathless and somehow dazzled. He felt that the sum total of his senses had been chopped into crazy little fragments, like torn paper, blowing away, scattered everywhere. He couldn't trust himself, didn't know what to do with himself.

When he got home he went straight to the bathroom and vomited. His mother took his temperature and decided that he had the flu. She put him to bed and fed him broth, and he was not allowed to spend Thanksgiving weekend with his father. The next time Brian put on his brown leather jacket, he found that the hole in the pocket had been mysteriously sewn up.

Chapter Eleven

Rachel could not decide about the tree, whether the lights should be all one color, or whether she should use a variety of colors. It was not a real tree this year. She felt a little bad about that, but real trees were so expensive. And a real tree would have implied something—a real celebration, an actual family get-together, which this was not. Christmas would be just like Thanksgiving; it would be Rachel and Brian together, formal and vaguely restless, doing random things and wondering where the meaning was.

It shouldn't be this way, she thought. I should do something about it. I should do something. She sat down on the sofa and stared at the small artificial tree she had purchased that afternoon. It was silver; even the base had been sprayed with silver paint and there were places on the sides of the base where the paint was splotchy and dull wood showed through.

In the store the tree hadn't looked half bad—it was bright and glittery; it fit in with all the tinsel and baubles crowding the store counters. There was artificial snow on the counters—thick sparkling stuff that was warm to the touch. The little silver tree had been sitting there in the warm snow, and she had gone over in a sudden gesture of enthusiasm. With a brief trembling of Christmas spirit, she had picked up the tree, brandishing it before the other shoppers like some sort of special promise. She went straight to the check-out stand, trying to keep this new feeling of satisfaction from dissolving. But the feeling was gone before she reached home.

Now, looking at the tree, Rachel had an impulse to laugh. The tree was funny, a regular riot. Hilarious. What kind of tree was this, anyway? It would get the gold lights, which it deserved—the ones that showed tarnished places. The bad spots would look like reflections, dark and a little muddled. No one would look close enough to see the bad places.

That decided, Rachel got up and walked across the room to inspect the tree from another angle. It looked the same—a simple matter of wires and cellophane and tin foil or something. She should have bought a regular tree, a real one that at least made the place look like Christmas. That's what she needed—a real tree.

She had been willing to go out to one of those lots where trees stood in great bunches, their branches lush, sweet and prickly. She was willing. She would have gone even to the mountains—to Big Bear perhaps—where they might have been able to cut down their own tree. Rachel was willing to do this and more, all for the sake of a tree, for the sake of Christmas. But Brian couldn't care less. Brian, who loved Christmas, said, "I don't care what you do. Do whatever you want. I don't have time to go running around looking for a tree."

So Rachel didn't care either—couldn't afford to care. The silver tree would do nicely. It was adequate. Perhaps it was better than the tree Jerry would have this year—if he bothered with a tree. She hoped he would. He needed something, a tree at least. It would be a ragged sort of bond between them—their own private, separate trees, just adequate.

Or would Jerry go all out and have a really magnificent tree? Would he invite her—that girl—to decorate it for him? What would they do? What would they do this Christmas?

Whenever Jerry came to see Brian, to pick him up and drive him off some place, he rarely said anything important to Rachel. His conversation was just so many words, small talk, little necessary connections linking this action to that. It was like a chain, a series of steps, everything in logical order: Jerry in the doorway greeting her; Jerry looking at his watch, hurrying Brian along; Jerry flashing that opaque smile that kept his thoughts private and mysterious; Jerry and Brian going out the door, the door shutting, and the sequence over, ended just like that.

This was Christmas Eve and Jerry might drop by. He might drop by tomorrow, Christmas. There would be the brief meaningless blocks of conversation between them, the overdone politeness, but it would be better than this silence in the walls. It would be better with Jerry here, but that was something she shouldn't think about. It was dangerous thinking like that.

Rachel stared coolly at the tree, staring it down, ridiculing it, reminding herself that she did not want a husband in the house who did not love her. She was better off without him. She would get better. Would God expect her to stay with a man who—Marlene said yes. Marlene said God would certainly want her to—

"For crying out loud, let's get some lights on this tree," Rachel said out loud. Her voice came back at her like wind; she sounded a little crazy talking to herself like that.

If only somebody would come over. Marlene said

77

she might stop by—she had a few gifts to bring over. She might be here at any time, any minute.

If only Brian were home—even Brian, who kept her at a distance now and never said words that meant anything. He was getting just like his father, closed up and involved in things that had nothing to do with her.

Rachel didn't really worry about Brian; he was a good boy. He was growing up. It was part of growing up to grow away from people. It was to be expected. Sometimes Rachel would try to imagine what Brian was doing when he was not at home or in school. Often when he walked in the door, she would say, "What did you do today, Brian?" He would grunt or scowl as if she had said something stupid.

She would ask him again, patiently, as if saying the words for the first time. "I was over at Ronnie's," he would reply. If she pursued the subject he would say, "We were listening to records," or "We were just talking," or "We just goofed around." She would nod uncertainly, wondering what she could do to open him up. She wondered why she let him get away with such evasive answers. Why didn't she make him talk, tell her something? Why didn't she? Maybe because of her own guilt, nameless and persistent. That was probably it. Yes.

The doorbell rang and Rachel answered it quickly, expectantly. This was Christmas Eve! Someone was here to see her. This was a time to be merry.

"Merry Christmas, Rachel!"

It was Marlene. She had too many presents in her arms and was dropping them. She was working hard to balance all the gifts in her arms at once. "Oh, I should have made two trips," she said.

"Come on in, don't just stand in the doorway," said Rachel, moving aside, offering her arms for some of the gifts. "Let me take some of those."

"They're all for you and Brian, believe it or not. I found all these little things I wanted to get, so I did—instead of one big thing. The most fun is opening the packages."

"That's the truth," said Rachel, putting the packages on the sofa. She glanced at her little silver tree, still not decorated. "I haven't got the tree finished yet. We'll just put these here for now," she said.

"Where did you get your tree?"

"Gemco's. This afternoon. I decided not to fuss with a real one."

"Well, I should have thought of something like that," said Marlene agreeably. She fussed with her packages, arranging them carefully on the sofa. "These are for Brian," she said, indicating one stack of gifts. She looked around. "Where is Brian?"

"Well, he's supposed to be home. He's over at Ronnie Mayhew's. I told him to come home early. After all, it is Christmas Eve."

"He's been over there quite a bit lately, hasn't he?" Marlene noted. "What do you think of that boy, Rachel?"

"Ronnie Mayhew? I don't know, Marlene. I can't say I like him. He's rather strange. I can't explain it. He puts on a facade, so that I'm not sure what he's really like."

"But Brian likes him?"

"Oh, yes. You should see it. Brian adores him, follows him around like a little puppy dog. Brian is sold on him."

"I suppose that's the important thing," said Marlene doubtfully.

"I suppose," Rachel agreed. "But I'm just as glad they don't spend too much time here. I'm afraid I really don't like that boy."

Marlene sat down on the sofa and began fussing once more with one of the packages, straightening a bow, fluffing it gently. "Maybe I shouldn't ask this—just say so," she said, "but is Brian going to see his dad this Christmas?"

"Sure, Marlene," replied Rachel, nodding. She sat down in the chair that had been Jerry's. "Brian will see his father. It wouldn't be Christmas otherwise, would it?" Rachel felt her face grow warm. Her cheeks were probably red; Marlene would see that she was flustered. She laughed, sounding nervous, even to herself. "Brian will spend part of Christmas with Jerry. I mean, I don't want to break up those two; they have their times together."

"How is Jerry, do you know?"

"Oh, he's doing all right. I guess he's kind of worried about his job right now. You know how things are in the aerospace industry. Jerry says the whole business is going right down the tubes. I don't know, but that's what he says. He says a lot of good guys have been laid off. Now they're out pounding the pavement."

"Does he think he might be next or something?"

"He didn't say that, but I suppose it's on his mind."

Marlene frowned briefly, but her expression softened as she said, "I want you to know, Rachel, that I'm praying for you and Jerry. I still believe things will work out for you two. I just know it."

Rachel nodded slightly, without conviction, and smiled. Her smile felt pasted on, not quite there. "I'm afraid that's just wishful thinking Marlene," she murmured.

"How have you been feeling?" Marlene asked. "You're starting to show, that's good. Have you started wearing maternity clothes yet?"

"No, well, I don't go out too much. I have all these old shirts of Jerry's. They're comfortable, so I wear them—just around the house, of course." Rachel paused, then added, "I've been feeling pretty good. I'm surprised I feel so good. Sometimes I don't even feel pregnant." She hesitated, wondering if she should go on with her thoughts. Might as well; Marlene might as well know how she felt. "You know, Marlene," she said gently, "sometimes I go for days without even thinking about the baby. The baby still doesn't mean anything to me. I don't think about the baby and I know it's not right, but sometimes I still don't really want it."

"Rachel, I know you won't regret keeping your baby. Wait till he starts kicking and you know he's there."

"Yes," she said, looking faintly distracted. "Yes, I suppose it will be different then."

A sound outside the door drew their attention—a scuffing of feet, a certain clicking. The door opened and Brian came in, his face flushed with something like merriment or wonder. He grinned, showing the neat line of his teeth. "Hi, Marlene, hi, Mom," he said, undoing his coat. "Merry Christmas. It won't be long now—"

"How come you're so late, Brian?" Rachel asked, her words separate and concise. "I told you to be home

81

early. What were you doing all this time?"

"Oh, Mom," he whined, sounding suddenly like an exasperated old man. "I was at Ronnie's, Mom. I told you where I was going."

"But I told you to be home early. What were you doing?"

"Goofing around, Mom. We were just goofing around, that's all." Brian gave a reluctant nod as if to excuse himself and went straight to his room, swiftly closing the door behind him.

Chapter Twelve

Her thoughts are running wild, straying off to no-where. There is a hall, certainly a hall, very long, very mysterious. It is like a throat, with the narrow inner warmth of a throat. She is dazed by the warmth, her eyes pressed up against the darkness. She runs against the darkness, a frenzied running, with her thoughts trailing like kite string. She keeps running. What is this mad-ness? She hears voices, pinpoints of sound, faint and distant, distressing somehow. The voices of men. What are they saying? She can do nothing about the voices; they terrify her. She is screaming: *Jerry, Brian, Jerry!*

Rachel woke with a start. She sat up, trembling, then lay back down, sighing relief. *A dream, a stupid, hideous dream*, she thought. *I have been dreaming, that's all—just dreaming!*

Rachel rolled over and stared at the clock on the night-stand. Nearly eight. Saturday morning. She lis-tened. The house was full of a silence that she recognized and accepted now—the lack of a man in the house, a man's sounds, his special noises that one takes for grant-ed when they are there and misses when they are gone.

There was another silence, too, which Rachel under-stood as Brian's absence. No doubt Brian had risen and dressed and left the house soundlessly, so that he would not disturb his mother. He had gone to Ronnie's or the two of them had gone off some place together doing who-knew-what as the day was just beginning. Brian would be gone until lunchtime, when he would suddenly appear, eat the meal Rachel provided, and then wait patiently, wordlessly, for his father to arrive for their regular weekend excursion. This had become the pattern of things, the Saturday pattern.

It was a dream, she thought again—the hall, the voices, the running. It was nothing; a dream. What did it mean? Nothing; nothing!

Rachel had no desire to get out of bed. Her body was heavy, sluggish; it kept her down, prevented her from walking light and free. She had been putting on too much weight lately—three pounds over the Christmas holidays, nearly two pounds a week during the month of January. This would have to stop; she must do better during February. How could she be putting on so much weight? The baby was only six months along. How big would she be by nine months?

For an instant, she recalled the woman in the doctor's office during her first visit. That woman, who had been due at any moment, had been no part of Rachel then, just an object of curiosity. Now Rachel felt as if she were that woman—or soon would be! Rachel could not escape this baby, could not stop the processes inside her that continued relentlessly day and night creating a baby for her. She was part of the process, had become the process. Her own identity was slipping away, losing itself to the baby, whatever the baby was.

The baby was no longer an idea in her mind, no longer a mere theory lacking physical substance. She could feel this baby—he had a lot to do and he did not want her to rest. It seemed that his legs and arms moved constantly; he was anxious to get going, to get things done. Sometimes Rachel would lie on her back very still, on the sofa or on her bed, and would watch with fascination the gentle rolling movements on the surface of her abdomen. The baby would shift and turn and make small hills and silly angles of her stomach. It awed her sometimes to think of this tiny baby inhabiting the most secret center of her body. How could such a thing be?

Rachel made herself get out of bed. The morning offered her nothing, but she had to face it. She had to do something with it, get it behind her, over and done with.

She thought again that she should contact the lawyer. She was always putting it off. She should go ahead and get the divorce. At least start things rolling. Make the first move. She considered this while she poured herself some coffee. She should get the divorce from Jerry and make the final break. Perhaps she would feel better. Perhaps her life would not seem so suspended, so flimsy. Perhaps life would take on some direction again. It was possible.

Of course, she was still dependent on Jerry for financial support, but after the baby came, she could go out and get a job. Women were doing it all the time. She could take care of herself—and of Brian and the baby. They would manage all right.

Rachel sipped her coffee and reasoned that, on the other hand, perhaps it was just as well to let Jerry take the first step. If he decided he wanted this girl, this Kit Cannon, let him get the divorce. Why should she do it for him?

Rachel frowned into her coffee. She hated herself when she was like this. Her bitterness was like a dark thread sewing up her emotions. All of her feelings were tainted by it. There was nothing she could do. She was trapped, and her senses grew murky trying to reason it out.

In her head, Rachel knew that she was a Christian. The Holy Spirit lived inside her, no one had to tell her this. But she also knew that the Holy Spirit was having a hard time saying anything to her now. She didn't seem able to listen. Where was He, the Holy Spirit, that He couldn't be heard? That His voice was so small, like an echo? Had she, Rachel, done this to Him? Was she stifling this Spirit inside her? What could she do about it? She was on a particular course, a certain inevitable track, and how could she change anything now?

Rachel had prayed for her husband for years. She had trusted God for his salvation. Now Jerry was all but out of her life; he was like a candle going out and almost gone. What could she possibly do about him now?

And Brian. She had taken Brian to church almost half his life (since he was eight). She had resolved that he would not be like his father, not an unsaved man like Jerry. She had done everything she could do. Now, Brian was slipping away, shutting her out, becoming a stranger to her. In January, he had given up his Sunday school office and his duties as social chairman of his youth group. He skipped church whenever possible, whenever Rachel would let him get away with it. When she forced him to go, he trudged silently behind her, like a sulking prisoner, a man condemned. How could this be? What terrible thing was wrong with Brian?

Rachel rinsed out her coffee cup and went into the living room to sit down. She was always tired now, needing to sit down frequently, needing to rest. She was constantly aware of her body—its demands, its pervading weaknesses, the overwhelming limitations of her body. Would she ever be free again? Would her spirit be free?

There was a brief stab of regret in Rachel's consciousness, a regret she could not define or touch with her thinking. It had something to do with her love for Christ and her inability to claim His power, the power He certainly wanted her to have. Why did she always fall so far short of what He wanted?

Rachel had not prayed for a very long time. She had occasionally mouthed prayers—glib phrases that fell into place without thought, small talk in the presence of God. She recognized the futility of such prayer, for the tone of her voice was much like the inevitable tone of the conversations she had with Jerry. Nothing real was ever said; nothing real was alluded to. Words skimmed the surface, rarely touching a significant base. It was that way now with God; she rarely touched base with Him, rarely made connections. Where was God that she could no longer reach Him?

She could attempt to pray. She could try to break through the wall she had built around herself, the willfulness and resentment of her own heart. She could do that.

"I don't know what to say," she thought, aware of a vague stirring of panic. What if she couldn't get through, could never again get through to God? Was she doomed to face all of the mornings of her life like this one—without meaning or purpose or joy? Gray, tasteless mornings? Was that her fate?

"Dear God," she said aloud, her voice filling up the silent spaces of the house. "Dear God, I don't know what to say to You anymore. I love You, but I don't know how to reach You. Help me, please help me."

There was a fragile responsiveness rising in her heart, a familiar sense of surrender beginning to wash over her. Good. It was working. Her prayers were working. Now, if only God would cleanse the corners and private recesses of her soul. Could it be that simple? Could she be clean again? Dear God, she longed to be clean.

Her words faltered. Her throat was closing up. She had nothing to give to God; there was no good in her. How could she pray? She tried to think of something worthwhile to say, but nothing came to mind. What was she thinking of, thinking she could ever please God? Why not give up, forget it, leave God alone? What had God to do with her?

Warm tears stuck to her lashes, spilling out. She brushed at them with her hand. Now she would have to blow her nose. Was there a Kleenex in her bathrobe pocket?

"Dear God, I'm sorry," she said, fumbling with the tissue, blowing her nose. "I need You so much, but I can't change anything myself. I can't reach You. Don't be a stranger to me, Father, please take charge; take control. I give You all that I am, the whole mess of my life. And I give you Jerry and Brian, too. They are strangers to me—we are all strangers. I can't handle it anymore. Do what You want with me, Lord."

For the entire morning, Rachel wept and prayed.

Chapter Thirteen

Marlene Benson opened a can of Campbell's chunky vegetable soup and emptied the contents into a saucepan on the stove. She added a little water, although this was not required. She turned on the gas so that a bright blue flame erupted under the saucepan, then stirred the water gently into the soup. She took a slice of bread from the freezer and set it on a plate to thaw. Marlene always kept a loaf in the freezer; this was the only way to keep it fresh, since she used only a slice or two at a time. Sometimes, a loaf of bread could last her two weeks or more.

Marlene set up a TV tray in front of the sofa in the living room. It was a flowered metal tray she had gotten with trading stamps—orange and yellow flowers, daisies or something. She checked the TV Guide to see what was on. There was one of those new programs about law and order, a crime drama, and a Ginger Rogers movie made in 1942. She chose the movie.

Marlene went back to her kitchen and spread diet margarine on the thawed bread. She was putting on a little weight again—she could feel a thickening around her waist and hips—so she would try a new diet, although she supposed it would last no longer than most of her self-imposed diets. She considered a moment and then yielded to the temptation to spread a generous layer of grape jelly on the bread.

Start the diet tomorrow, she thought. She could be

quite philosophical about it, for there was really no one who would notice—or who cared—whether she lost or gained 10 pounds. It was possible that someone from church or at work would look her up and down and exclaim, "Oh, Marlene, dear, you're putting on weight," or "Why, Marlene, you look thinner, how marvelous!" But more likely no one would say anything one way or the other, whether she looked like a blimp or like Twiggy. So the jelly really didn't matter.

There was a pattern to Marlene's days, a strict routine that rarely varied, the sort of schedule people living alone set for themselves. She probably would have denied it with an alarmed wave of the hand, for she liked to think of herself as free to choose how her life would be and what she would do each day. Nevertheless, she rarely changed the sequence of her activities or the time delegated to each activity.

Marlene was free in one sense, for she had no one to please but herself, no one to make concessions to, since that dreadful day her husband died in the factory accident, that terrible explosion. Since then there had been no one but herself.

Well, she reflected with some amusement, there was someone, or could be; but he hardly counted. In fact, he probably didn't even know Marlene's last name—to show how much he counted! But she cared for him—Mr. Timmons, Stanley Timmons, was an usher from the church. He was a pleasant-faced, rather shy middle-aged bachelor with thin wisps of graying hair and round, black, plastic-rimmed glasses sliding halfway down his nose. Marlene often felt an impulse to push his glasses up for him to the top of his nose, but since their conversation was usually limited to a formal "good morning" or "good evening, how are you tonight?"—she would surely never attempt such a thing.

Periodically Marlene prayed that Mr. Timmons might notice her and realize what fine qualities she possessed—that it might suddenly dawn on him that here was the kind of Christian woman he needed. Still Mr. Timmons offered her only a rather stiff "Good morning" each Sunday before passing out of her life for another week. Each week she put her all into that "Good morning, Mr. Timmons, how are you today?"—but for naught. It was rather hopeless, she thought dismally, taking mouthfuls of soup.

This night was like any other night, like *every* other night for Marlene—eating her dinner while watching TV, nothing expected of her, no one demanding anything in particular, the whole world leaving her to the quietness of walls and overstuffed furniture. Her life was like a record being played over and over—the same quiet dinners and TV and her own private thoughts going over the day, wondering about all the days ahead; the same thoughts played over and over, different and still the same.

Marlene Benson had a particular closeness to God that prevented her from feeling her life was meaningless. If anything, she considered herself in a state of waiting, of suspension perhaps. At any moment, at the signal of the Lord Himself, the waiting would be over, things would click into place and the wheels of her life would begin to revolve. She was certain of this and waited for it patiently.

In the meantime, she kept busy; and she accomplished a great many things. She worked as an executive secretary for a plastics firm in downtown Long Beach.

She was Sunday school teacher for eighth grade girls and was on several of the committees for the Women's Fellowship and the Missionary Guild. She had a full life—people would certainly agree she had enough to keep her busy.

Marlene enjoyed being busy and she enjoyed people. She had always been considered somewhat aggressive, an extrovert, never at a loss for words, ready for anything, a good sport. Good old Marlene. She could be counted on, Marlene could. She always did her part, did what she felt were her duties before God. But as the years passed, especially since her husband's death, she became increasingly aware of the fact that she was more comfortable with God than she was with people.

Around other people it was necessary to be many things—neat, attractive, polite, saying and doing whatever was appropriate for the persons and circumstances involved. Marlene had never found it easy to be attractive. Comical, the life of the party, someone's big sister, all of these, yes. But attractive—no. She had never felt attractive. And though she ritualistically followed the rules of good grooming, she never escaped a certain sense of awkwardness, a feeling that something about her body was not quite right. She ignored the feeling, lived with it, laughed at it.

However, only when she was alone with God could she feel lusciously content. Accepted. When she prayed, she was beautiful; she knew it. She felt beautiful before God, and the thought of it warmed her. She knew this was merely a glimpse of how it would be in heaven when she had her transformed body, and this too was something she must wait for. In the meantime, she loved the Lord with a fierce devotion and waited for the things she knew would come to her.

This particular night was a slightly foggy February night, quiet except for the occasional muted blasts of a foghorn from the harbor. It was less than a week before St. Valentine's Day. On Valentine's Day, at seven in the evening, there would be a sweetheart banquet in the Christian education building adjoining the church—$3 per person, with an appetizing menu including veal and peas and mashed potatoes with gravy. The special guest speaker was a missionary on furlough from the Philippines. Perhaps Mr. Timmons would attend the banquet. Perhaps he would sit near her. Perhaps they would talk. Perhaps—or he might not come at all. She would not think of that.

It was Marlene's responsibility to prepare name cards for the sweetheart banquet. She had colored paper and scissors and black marking pens ready. She had a list of names of people who had signed up to attend. Mr. Timmons' name was not on the list, but that meant nothing. Only that he had not given the church secretary his name, that he had not yet purchased his ticket. He had time—a week. She had time; she was good at waiting.

Marlene was sorting the sheets of colored paper when she heard the first sound—a car pulling up outside, the engine turned off. She ignored it, busy with her paper. She was expecting no one; the sound was forgotten. Then, five minutes or ten minutes later, Marlene heard the slamming of a car door. This was nothing either. Car doors slammed all the time. But then, something else: a shuffling of feet, footsteps on the sidewalk, a sound at her door, a sudden insistent knocking. Marlene jumped up, startled, and dropped the colored paper on the desk.

"Who—?" she said. She moved toward the door, listening. The pounding stopped for a moment, then began again, harder and demanding.

Marlene felt an unreasonable fear shoot through her chest. She quelled the fear, pushing it out of her mind—it was nothing at all, this absurd noise. In spite of herself, she felt weak. She would have to tell her arms what to do, make them move. She listened, wondering what was happening, what would happen next. No one ever came to see her with such hard pounding on her door. People who came to see her knocked gently, a careful, pleasant knock with pauses between, so that she could answer. No one ever wanted her enough to bang so heavily, with such apparent intensity. What was going on?

Marlene slipped the chain lock into place on the door and peered through a narrow slit in the curtains. A man stood outside. It was too dark to determine his identity, but something in his stance suggested Jerry Webber. Marlene peeked again. Yes. Yes, Jerry Webber. What did he want? She opened the door a crack. The chain lock was in place. She said softly, "Jerry? Jerry Webber? Is that you out there?"

Was he startled by her voice? He moved backward suddenly, stepping awkwardly. "What? Jerry Webber, you say? Why, you bet! This is Jerry Webber all right. What you got the door locked for?"

"I didn't know who was knocking—"

"Me! I was knocking. Where were you? I kept knocking—"

"I'm sorry, Jerry. What do you want?"

"Want? I want in—let me in, Marlene. I want to talk

94

"Laid off? Yeah, laid off—like Russian roulette. I knew my turn was coming. It was just a matter of time, that's all. That's all anything is—a matter of time."

"You're sure you don't want some coffee?"

"No coffee! I said no coffee, didn't I? A man loses everything he ever had and people want to give him coffee. What is this—coffee? Why coffee?"

"Does Rachel know about your job?"

"No. What's it to her? Money? I'll get money for her. I'll find something, some job."

"I'm sorry, Jerry. I don't know what to say—"

"Say nothing. What's it to you? You and Rachel—what do either of you have to do with me? I don't know why I came here."

"I wish I could help—"

"Oh, you helped all right, baby. You helped a long time ago when you filled Rachel's head with all that garbage. Religion, church, believe this, believe that. She was fine until you came along—fine, I tell you."

It seemed to Marlene that Jerry had been sounding off to the walls, staring holes in the plaster, a terrible anger clouding his eyes. But now he stopped and stared at her, looked imploringly at her, like a dying man might look, like a man full of unspeakable anguish. "What did you do to her, Marlene?" he asked, the words catching somewhere in his throat. "She never came back, never came back to me after she got mixed up with you. What did you do?"

"I didn't do anything, Jerry," Marlene answered, groping for words. "I just showed her how to accept Christ as her Savior, that's all I did."

"She never came back, not really. She was never the same."

"That had nothing to do with me, Jerry. God changed her. She gave herself to God. That made the difference."

"That made her shut me out? What kind of God is that, breaking up families, wrecking homes? Answer me that, will you?"

"But Jerry, Rachel wanted you to share her faith. She wanted that more than anything in the world."

"She took Brian and the two of them went their own way. Sometimes I almost hated her; it bugged me to think I wasn't the most important thing in her life anymore. I couldn't compete with this God of hers; how could I compete? I was a poor second, that's what I was. There was always this barrier between us."

"It didn't have to be that way, Jerry. It doesn't have to be now. Christ loves you as much as He loves Rachel."

"No, don't start on me, Marlene. I don't want to hear it. This God of yours, this loving God, took everything away from me—my home, my wife, my son, and now my job. What kind of God is that? I think your God would like to finish me off, that's what I think."

"You feel that way because you're beating your head against Him, and against His love," said Marlene softly. "If you would just accept His love! He's trying to reach you. These things that have happened are God's way of getting your attention, making you realize your need—"

"My need is to get out of here," he shouted hoarsely. He got up and headed for the door. "You're crazy, you're a crazy woman," he said, fumbling with the doorknob.

"Jerry, please, listen to me. When you're sober, go

see the pastor at our church. Dr. Emrick. Go talk to him. Maybe he can help you understand. Do you hear me, Jerry? Jerry!"

He stormed out the door, slamming it behind him. "Crazy, crazy woman," Marlene heard him exclaim to the night.

Chapter Fourteen

It was the first of March, a cool evening. The air was very still. Jerry Webber unlocked the door to his apartment and went in, flicking the light switch as he entered. The overhead bulb jarred away the darkness and bathed the room with a smooth sallow light that brought things into focus. The room smelled stale, closed up; it was a dark box that shunned air.

Jerry removed his coat and slipped it over a hanger in the closet, straightening the collar and the sleeves. Somehow the material felt worn and sleazy, although it was an expensive coat.

This place was an eyesore, a cheap one-bedroom furnished apartment, something he could afford. The furniture was light and colorless, having no personality, mere sticks of polished wood arranged and fastened with glue in angles resembling furniture—a chair, a sofa, end tables. Jerry had as little to do with this place as he could; he did not allow himself to become a part of it. When he sat down, he remained on the surface, not relaxing, not letting himself find comfort in this furniture that was not his own. This was not home, nothing like his home.

Somewhere else, only miles away, was his home, a place that was still part of him, though he did not belong there now. In that other place were his wife and son, going about their business, doing the things people do everyday—without him. He—Jerry Webber—had been relegated to this place.

Since he had moved to this apartment—what was it? four months ago?—he had spent hours in this new place, hating it, fearful that somehow it might become a permanent thing, a place he would never escape.

Thinking about it now, he could almost be amused; he could almost smile at the dread he had had of these rooms. Now, tonight, this fine March night, even the dreariness of the walls did not bother him. He was immune. He could walk through the rooms of this place and not be touched. He would not suffocate. He was breathing, and he would not have to worry about his breath again.

He was free and did not even know yet what it meant—free!

Bound by the limitations of his body and his mind and this apartment; feeling keenly the loss of Rachel and his son and his job; his dignity and his selfhood threatened and his future hanging by a thread—still, he was free. What did that mean? What really did it mean? Free.

Jerry went to the kitchen for a glass of milk. He took the milk and a box of crackers with him to the living room and sat down. The crackers were slightly stale, and made no sound when he ate them. This place that he hated was silent for a change, silent in all of its parts, waiting for him to sort and arrange all his thoughts. This apartment would not threaten him again, he knew that. That part of his life was over—the threat of things that might devour him, of things that had no end.

He thought back, going over the day's chain of events, the innocuous activities leading up without warning to this new thing, this sudden freedom he could not comprehend. He remembered that the day had started badly. He had nothing to do, no reason for getting out of bed. It was getting to him—this having no job—it was getting him down. He was displaced and floating, with no strings to tie him to anything. He needed ties but there was nothing, only the irrelevant continuity of days and nights—days without meaning, nights without rest. And the needs, endless and vaguely disturbing—the need to eat, to shave, to dress and undress, and the need to come to something at last, to make some sense of being a man, of living.

He wondered what had brought him to this place where he was now, to this empty endless moment with its terrible demands? What had brought him here and what could he do about it? Or was he helpless, destined forever to be a 35-year-old man with no home, no family and no peace?

Those had been his thoughts this morning. He had shaved and dressed, his mind sullen, his body sluggish, like an old man who had nowhere to go. Why should he be like an old man to whom everything in life had already happened? He fixed breakfast for himself—bacon and eggs and coffee—although he was not hungry and had no desire for the taste of food.

He left his apartment before noon and went to the corner for a newspaper. It was a ritual. He scanned the classified ads, his eyes moving hungrily down each column. There was nothing for him; he did not really expect anything. Rumor was that hundreds of engineers were applying for a single civil service job, or any job—a gardener, clerk, filling station attendant. Jerry suspected the rumors were true. No one wanted engineers.

When he had finished with the morning paper each day, he went for a walk, as if he actually had somewhere to go. Some days he drove around to various companies in the area, going in the door with a confident stride, asking the receptionist if he could see the personnel man. Or could he fill out an application or leave his resume?

The girls who greeted him were always polite. They listened, watching him with clear, alert eyes. They took his resumes and let him take application blanks to fill out. But their smiles said there was nothing. They could afford such charity, for they knew what he knew: he was wasting his time. Nevertheless, he appreciated their smiles and returned them generously, maintaining for these girls a facade of optimism.

Today, however, he would not play that game. He would not go through the motions. Instead, he walked and let his thoughts carry him where they would. He thought a great deal about his life and about his wife and son. It bothered him that not only had his own life been upset by the events of the last few months, but his wife and son had been wounded deeply as well.

It seemed he hardly knew Rachel now since their separation. She avoided him, demonstrating a coldness he knew sprang from the hurt she felt. And the knowledge that she had been desperate enough at one point to consider an abortion was more painful than Jerry cared to admit. But that was in the past now. Rachel would be all right. She would manage.

But what about Brian? He had changed during the past few weeks, in ways Jerry could not explain. On the surface they got along, talked, had a good time together. But on another level, Brian was different, older, growing increasingly remote.

Besides, there had been incidents that had raised nagging questions in Jerry's mind. For instance, the day he picked Brian up at school to take him to visit the Queen Mary. Brian had become sick and had to go home. Was it really just something he had eaten? Or could it have been something else? Did Jerry only imagine the signs?

Then there was the evening he and Brian were having a purely academic discussion about the legalization of marijuana. They were drinking McDonald's milk shakes and munching fries when a news blurb on the subject came over the radio. In minutes, Brian's face became animated and his voice rose heatedly. Why should the possession of marijuana be an illegal act? How was pot really any worse than cigarettes or liquor? Why couldn't people decide for themselves what they wanted to do?

Jerry, hiding his surprise and concern, remarked only that he hoped Brian would never get involved in drugs. When Brian made no attempt to reply, Jerry persisted. He hoped Brian would have the good sense to leave drugs alone. What tormented Jerry since that evening was that Brian never gave him an answer, never said a word. Jerry was left with his own nagging, growing suspicions. Did Brian need help? What could Jerry do?

As Jerry continued to walk, his thoughts turned to the baby, a child destined to be a stranger to him. What could he do for this child when he could not even help himself? Soberly, thoughtfully, Jerry considered the entire pattern of his life, going step by step over all the events that had brought him to this present moment.

He reflected that he had done a great deal with his life and yet now he had nothing. It was as if he had to start all over, building a new identity, a new man to take the place of Jerry Webber. But how could he do this? He was who he was—the result of 35 years' experiences, the product of his own actions and attitudes.

He realized dismally that he could not unwrap a single hour of his life and rewrap it into a different mold with a new, more pleasing shape. He could change nothing of the past; he was locked into the present moment. Already the future was slipping over him, confusing him—a filmy web of weird mosaics. By the time he was freed from the tangle of it all, it would be gone, dissolved, just more of the past to puzzle over and finally forget. Things were inevitable, the whole course of life. There was only so much anyone could do. It was never enough.

Jerry had walked this afternoon until his feet hurt. At last he had given up and gone back to his apartment to sit by the window looking out, waiting for something, anything, to happen. He thought about the day he was laid off (was it really less than a month ago, not years?), the shock of it, that he could actually be one of the guys laid off. The astonishment persisted, even now, buried somewhere. Why had it been such a shock?

He thought about the fact that Kit had not been laid off. She was still needed. They had work for her to do, and—it was funny—work was not really important to Kit. She was conscientious, going each day to the office and doing her work well, but she would just as soon not have worked at all, if she didn't have to. Funny, yes.

Jerry had not seen much of Kit lately. What was there to say to her? What was the use of seeing her? After he and Rachel separated, he had dated Kit occasionally, but their relationship didn't seem to be going anywhere. It baffled him. He had been on the verge of falling in love with her and had admitted as much to Rachel. But then, something happened; nothing happened. What was it? Was it that he could not commit himself? Was he unwilling to push his life impulsively into some new mold when all of the separate parts of his life were so unsettled? He could love Kit, but did he want that love to take charge of him, possess him?

Kit had seemed to sense Jerry's confusion; she had left him to himself and, during office hours, had remained friendly and completely unruffled. But now that he no longer saw her at the office, there seemed even less reason to see her socially. Perhaps someday when things were straightened out—

Jerry spent the afternoon thinking about being laid off, recalling how he stalked out of the office that terrible day and headed for the nearest bar. Marco's Tavern was just down the block from work; it was a place he disliked and rarely visited, but it was a place where he could get stoned when he had to forget something as bad as losing a job.

He had sat in the cool murky darkness of that place for hours, drinking beer at first, and then, because beer hadn't done the job, he had ordered whiskey. He drank until he felt the need to go to the bathroom, and then, leaving the john, he glanced into a dirty, smudged mirror and saw the grotesqueness of his face, the swelling around his eyes, a puffiness he detested. He had the look of a crazy man, a man who had lost the ability to reason. He remembered now how it startled him to see himself like that, how he had gone out quickly, nearly running to his car, ashamed somehow of his image in the mirror.

He had driven to his old apartment, where Rachel

and Brian lived. He sat in the car in front of the apartment house nearly half an hour, dazed, his thoughts muddled. He realized he could not go to Rachel, but he had driven to this place. Why? What was here for him?

At last he had gotten out of the car and had gone to the door of the downstairs apartment, where Marlene Benson lived. He had pounded on the door, shouting, needing to be heard. Haltingly, with trepidation, Marlene had taken him in, had listened to him and talked to him. What had she said? It was fuzzy; nothing she said remained with him, except one thing: she had begged him to go see her pastor. Talk to him, she said.

The idea remained lodged somewhere in Jerry's head; and so this afternoon, while he sat by the window looking out, waiting for something to happen —on this fine March day the memory of her words came to him, and he thought, *"That is something I can do!"*

Now it was evening. He was in his apartment, sitting on his sofa eating stale crackers and drinking milk, marveling over the fact that he was finally free. He was still in a state of astonishment, dazed at what he had done. How had it come about—this new freedom? How did it happen?

He considered the evening, savoring the memory of the last few hours. Earlier this evening he had gone to see Dr. Emrick, Marlene and Rachel's pastor, and had sat with him in his study for several hours, telling this man he hardly knew the whole story of his life. And when it had come time for Dr. Emrick to speak, something had happened inside Jerry. For the very first time, he understood. It wasn't his imagination. He was responding to the verses the minister read from the Bible.

At first he was mildly surprised at himself, at the receptiveness he felt inside. What was going on, that suddenly he had an appetite for this sort of thing—for religion, for God?

Then the response expanded. As the pastor explained the way of salvation and told him about the Person of Jesus Christ, Jerry was aware of a hunger sweeping over him, stretching through his mind, absorbing his entire imagination. He was convinced now that he had a soul, for this idea of Christ saving him had electrified an unknown part of him. The sensation pleased and intrigued him.

He accepted the pastor's suggestion that they kneel and pray together, that Jerry ask Christ into his heart and life and claim Christ's gift of eternal life. It was done in a moment and Jerry got off his knees without a word and with little emotion in him.

There was instead within his mind a lucidity, a clarity of perception, a certain recognition of something vital. He had finally found an answer, *the* Answer. All of his life, the meaning of living had escaped him. Life was a puzzle. Men could assemble many pieces of it in a lifetime, coming up with various meanings as the pieces fit together. But no man could see the entire picture or learn the essential meaning of life until he grasped the one piece that made the puzzle complete. Why had he never seen it before? Christ was the missing piece, the all-important key. Without Him life was incomplete; the meaning of living could not be comprehended. Now, for the first time, Jerry had the whole picture. He had all the pieces; all the pieces fit!

Into Jerry's mind flashed a clear image of something

from a book he had read in school as a youngster—John Bunyan's *The Pilgrim's Progress*. He recalled that Christian carried a heavy burden on his back, his load of sins; but as soon as he reached the cross, the burden tumbled from his shoulders, and Christian was light and free and joyful. The story had always amused Jerry a little, for certainly, life was not like that; he hadn't even sensed he carried any burden back then.

Now, however, having claimed the blood of Christ for the atonement of his own sins, he had to admit to a certain sensation of lightness and liberty. He was a new man in Christ. He rejoiced in his heart. It was a fact. He was free.

Jerry Webber returned the box of stale crackers and the empty milk glass to the kitchen, marveling as he went at his new freedom, his salvation. Imagine it, imagine being free.

Chapter Fifteen

Jerry glanced at his watch. Not quite seven. Might know, he'd be early. Too bad, Kit was not known for her promptness. He would probably have to wait for her, sitting around while she fussed with her makeup or something. He wanted to get on with this evening. There were things he had to say to Kit, things she would have to know. He didn't want to waste time on trifles, not tonight.

Rapping on her apartment door, he thought ruefully that it would be just his luck for Kit's roommate to be home. She was a pain, that girl. She never shut up. He hoped she was off somewhere for the evening. Jerry needed peace tonight so that he could keep his thoughts in order. He had certain things he needed to say.

The door opened. Sure enough, it was Kit's roommate. "Hi, Jerry, come on in," she chirped. "You're early, aren't you? Kit mentioned 7:30—" Joyce Barnes—or Burns, he could never remember which— was a lanky blonde with an unstylish bouffant hairdo. She wore thick orange lipstick and false eyelashes that never seemed to be quite in place.

"I said, come on in," she said, her voice high, a little shrill. "I can't help you; I just did my nails. Like?" She held out her hands, spreading her fingers in the air. She blew on them. "The stuff's called 'pink passion' or something, can you believe it? Actually, the nails are fake. I bite mine to the quick."

He followed Joyce into the room. "Is Kit ready?"

"Ready? Are you kidding me? You could get here an hour late and you'd still have to wait. She just got out of the tub."

From another room, Jerry heard Kit's voice. "Is that you, Jerry? Be with you in a minute. Keep him entertained, Joyce."

"You want a beer?" asked Joyce, turning toward the kitchen.

"No, no thanks."

"No? Okay, I'll skip it too. I don't need it anyway. Too many calories."

Jerry let the girl's words rush somewhere over his head. People like Joyce irritated him. She was a flurry of nervous energy, constantly waving her arms around absurdly. He didn't attempt to make sense of this girl. Was there anything real beneath her jangly, brash, agitated exterior? He recalled that Kit said Joyce was a receptionist somewhere. He couldn't imagine where.

She was bubbling on about something, a movie she and Kit had seen, somebody in the movie she especially liked. Automatically, Jerry smiled or nodded or shook his head when he thought it was expected of him. He was polite. Certainly he could be polite. But he wished Kit would hurry. He realized now that he should have walked around the block or stopped for coffee somewhere—anything to kill time. Just to be some place where he didn't have to listen.

"Sit down, Jerry, come on. For heaven's sake, relax," said Joyce cheerfully, as if the idea of sitting down had sprung upon her unexpectedly. "Don't wait for me

112

to think of it," she said, laughing. She sat down on the couch and patted a space beside her, coaxing him. "You like Walter Cronkite, don't you?" She nodded toward the TV. "The color's not right, do you notice it? The faces are yellow. I think a tube's gone bad. Do you know anything about televisions?"

"No," he said vaguely, sitting down where Joyce indicated. He was having a difficult time focusing his thoughts on what she was saying. Cronkite? Yes, he liked Cronkite. No, he knew very little about television sets.

"I was watching the eyewitness news earlier tonight, and they were interviewing Ronald Reagan. I think he's really cute, but of course he should have stayed on the late show, don't you think?"

"I don't know, Reagan's all right," he said, thinking of something else.

"Oh, sure, I suppose," she agreed brightly. "Say, you sure you don't want some beer? We got pretzels too."

He came back to himself, forgetting whatever it was he was thinking of. "Joyce, really, nothing for me," he said, trying to convince her. "Kit and I will be eating out."

"Oh, yeah, sure," she said. She seemed distracted now. "You don't mind if I smoke, do you?" she asked. She looked at him blankly, a little perturbed perhaps, and asked, "Have you got a cigarette on you? I'm all out."

"No, I don't."

She shrugged. "Oh, well, that's okay. This girl at work calls them 'cancer sticks.' She says I smoke too much. So I die young. So what? No one lives forever, I say."

Jerry smiled. "I don't know about that—"

"Say, I'm going out to dinner tonight too, believe it or not," said Joyce. She gave her nails an appraising look. "This guy I'm dating works the night shift, but he's off early tonight. He parks cars at this restaurant in Torrance. He's from Bellflower originally, a native Californian, how about that? He was over in Vietnam when we were getting out. He stayed right to the end, helping to evacuate all those refugees. To this day he can't forget it. That was some experience, I tell you!" Jerry watched as the girl carefully inspected one long pink fingernail. "Almost lost it," she said, sighing something like relief.

Kit finally came breezing into the room, smelling of perfume and hair spray. Jerry slipped her coat around her shoulders and quickly guided her out the door. He got her into the car and climbed in on his side, fastening his seat belt. He looked at her and wondered suddenly what to say. There were remnants of feeling for her still inside him, vague memories of desire, a certain impulse to act out of habit—to kiss her, touch her face, her hands. He realized he had to construct a new set of reactions. This was the beginning of something new—or more accurately, the end of something old. He was not sure what the purpose of this evening was. He would tell Kit of the change within him; he wanted to share this new joy with her. And he would have to tell her it was over between them, this thing that had never really begun.

"Hungry?" he asked, working with his keys, pushing the proper key into the ignition.

"I guess so, yeah. How about you?"

"Sure, famished," he said. What kind of inane conversation was this? He started the car and pulled out into the street.

"It's been a long time," she said lightly.

He agreed with a slight nod of the head, not looking her way. He steered through heavy traffic and finally entered a freeway on-ramp. "How are things at work?" he asked. Work was a harmless topic.

"All right, I guess. There's really not much work. They lost out on some more government contracts and laid off a few more guys out in the shop. We scratch around for things to do, really." She shifted in the seat, turning slightly so that she could look at him. "How about you, Jerry?" she said. "Have you found anything yet?"

"A job? No, nothing yet. I've contacted some agencies back East, and, of course, I've made the rounds out here—but you know how things are in aerospace right now."

"I know," she said sadly. "It's a real bummer, isn't it?"

"Well—" he hesitated. "At least some things in my life are on the upswing."

She gave him a penetrating glance. "You mean, your wife?"

"Oh, no. I don't mean Rachel. There's nothing new there." He smiled briefly at her, observing that her eyebrows were perfect. There was a translucence to her face, a kind of sheen. She was wearing a light green dress, velvet perhaps or something similar, stylish and really very pretty. Her legs were crossed at the knee, graceful legs, long and smooth. Abruptly Jerry cut off his thoughts, suspending them sharply in mid-air. He reminded himself that Kit was a closed door to him now.

There would be nothing between them. He had decided that.

"What do you mean then?" she asked.

"Well, things are getting better."

"In what way?"

"That's what I wanted to talk to you about. I thought we could talk over dinner."

"Why dinner? Why not now? Why not tell me now?" she asked, teasing gently, prodding him.

"I thought we could go out to that Mexican restaurant on Atlantic. We went there once before, remember?"

"All right."

"That is, if you're hungry for Mexican food . . ."

"Sure, fine."

"They have great guacamole salad, remember?"

"Jerry, don't put me off," Kit insisted. "I don't like it. I said we could talk right now. Why not right now?"

"Maybe you won't want to go out to dinner with me after we talk," he said pleasantly, testing her.

"Try me," she said.

"Okay, Kit. Here it is," he replied. "We won't be seeing each other anymore."

"All right."

"*All right?* I don't understand."

"I knew this was coming, Jerry. It just figured. In my head, I already knew."

Jerry felt baffled, a little put down. "How did you know? I mean, *I* didn't know."

Kit's voice was plain, matter-of-fact. "You kept me at arm's length, Jerry. You wouldn't get involved. We never had a chance. I figured it. I'm not surprised."

"I told you before, Kit, I couldn't get involved until I

could commit myself, until I knew where I was going."

"And you know now?"

"Yes, I do; I finally do."

"And this commitment doesn't include me at all, does it, Jerry." It was not a question but a statement.

"Not the way you think, not the way we hoped. There can't be anything between us, Kit, because the whole direction of my life has changed."

"Hey, that's heady stuff, Jerry," she said.

"Yeah." He smiled, relaxing a little. "Kit," he said gently, his voice light, "I don't want to spout platitudes. That's not my style, believe me. Well, you know me; I don't have to tell you how I am."

"No."

"But something happened to me, Kit, and this I do have to tell you."

"What do you mean?"

"I can't put words around it, Kit. I can't give it a definition. There's no label for it. All I want you to know is that Jesus Christ isn't just a name or a swear word to me anymore. He's a living person, and He's done something for me I can't begin to understand. I mean, Kit, it's like falling in love, like being set free."

"You mean, you've joined Rachel's church? You're converting to her religion?"

"No, not exactly. I'm talking about being committed to a person, to God Himself—personally. I know Jesus Christ, His Spirit. How can I explain it to you? As far as church is concerned, I haven't really thought yet about a church. I suppose now I should—"

"You know what you sound like, Jerry? You know what you remind me of?"

"What?"

"I met some Jesus freaks on Sunset Strip one night a couple years ago. They were singing and handing out papers and stuff. They were really turned on—and I don't mean drugs. Jerry, is that the sort of thing you're mixed up in? I mean, that stuff is far out."

"It's not really, Kit. I wish you could experience it. It's as if I've been going in circles all my life, like a whirling dervish or something, and now for the first time I've stopped—and I can see things clearly, I mean, real things. And it's beautiful."

"That's nice, Jerry, for *you*." Kit sounded unconvinced, detached, her voice flat. Jerry could sense that her mind was pulling away, erecting a barrier between them.

"I'd like to tell you more about it, Kit," he said tentatively.

"No, Jerry. I get the message. I don't mind; I understand. At least, I sort of understand. I don't dig the religion thing, that I don't get. But I expected the rest. I took a chance and lost. It really doesn't matter. I see to it that nothing matters too much."

"I'm sorry, Kit. I'm really sorry. I just wish there was something I could do."

Kit laughed—a brilliant, excited laugh. "Jerry," she said brightly, "I'm starved, really I am. Where is that fabulous restaurant anyway?"

Jerry drove on to the restaurant in silence.

He knew for a fact that only the Spirit of God could reach Kit Cannon.

Chapter Sixteen

What does a woman do when her husband goes away and does not come back? If she knows he is involved with another woman, how does she feel, left alone with her thoughts for days and months? If she is like Rachel she gets into a rut thinking nothing exists, not even her own body, her unborn child, or her own soul. She loses touch with God although she tries again and again to reach God, to make Him real.

What if this woman gets a call one day from her husband who wants to talk with her—not with Brian, their son, but with her? He has something very important to tell her. How does she feel, knowing this?

She marvels at the feeling—the silent, secret, remote joy, the slivers of excitement and growing anticipation—as she replaces the telephone receiver into its cradle. Like a woman in a dream, she goes straight to her room and changes her dress and freshens her face and brushes her hair. She inspects her image in the mirror, scrutinizing, slightly critical of the swelling of her body, the heaviness. Yet she is somehow pleased. She stares at herself in the glass—her eyes, her brows, her slender neck; and she wonders what it means. She has been trying too hard, too long, to make sense of her life. She knew the answers once; obviously she did. Where are the answers now?

Her husband will be here to see her. At any moment

he will arrive. He has something to say. Perhaps she will find answers in his words. Perhaps her husband will come with words to make things real.

The doorbell rang. Once. Twice. Rachel went to answer it, breathless with hurrying, breathless with expectancy. What did she expect? What could Jerry possibly have to say that would make any difference to her? It was too late for words. Words meant nothing. Words were not real.

She opened the door.

"Hello, Rachel. I hope I'm not too early."

"No, of course not. I told you to come right over. Come in." She directed him inside and invited him to sit down. It was like a ritual, an exercise in formality. He chose his old chair; she took the couch.

"How have you been feeling, Rachel?" he asked.

"Not too bad," she said, her voice light. "I'm awfully tired lately, but the doctor says that's normal, with the baby due in six weeks. I think the baby must weigh a ton, he's so heavy. I waddle now instead of walk." She smiled slightly, averting her eyes, feeling somehow embarrassed.

"You look good, Rae. You really do."

"Thank you."

"How's Brian?"

"All right, I suppose." She hesitated. "Did he tell you that he's been having some problems with school?"

Jerry's face registered surprise. "What kind of trouble?"

"Nothing serious, I guess. Mainly his grades. He's been getting C's and D's."

"He always got A's and B's before."

"Yes, something's wrong," she admitted. Her voice

was beginning to feel strangled. Was she going to cry? "I can't reach him anymore, Jerry. I can't say anything to him."

"I didn't realize it was that bad."

"Haven't you noticed a change in him?"

"Yes, I suppose I have, but he's always cheerful when we go out. He always seems to enjoy being with me. I had hoped I was only imagining a change."

"Well, Brian just sulks around me. He has nothing to say. He hangs around with Ronnie Mayhew and won't tell me what they do. I can hardly get him to go to church anymore."

"You mean he's stopped going to church?"

"Practically. I don't know anymore whether to twist his arm or just give in and leave him home."

"That's what I wanted to talk to you about."

"You mean Brian? Brian going to church?" she asked, puzzled.

"No. I mean, we will have to discuss Brian and church, but I wanted to talk about something else having to do with church."

"I don't understand. You sounded so urgent on the phone."

"Rachel, I went to see your pastor last week."

"Dr. Emrick?"

"We had a long talk. We talked for a whole evening."

"Why did you go see Dr. Emrick?"

"I was terribly depressed," Jerry replied. "You know I lost my job, Rae. It seemed like there was nothing left." He hesitated, staring at her, apparently trying to read her expression. "I suppose Marlene told you how I barged in on her—drunk."

"Yes, she told me."

"I think I really frightened her. She told me to go see your pastor. I thought of what she said a few weeks later and decided to do it. I didn't know what else to do. I was at the end of my rope."

"I'm sorry, Jerry. I didn't realize—"

"It's all right," he said. "I had to come to the end of myself before I was ready to look for an answer outside myself."

"What happened?"

"You know how I've despised the mess the world's in—the economy, pollution, political turmoil, crime, dope, racism, all the ugly things in this world. Well, Dr. Emrick showed me how all the evils of life are the result of sin, and sin starts with the individual, with me. I felt trapped and burdened because I was a sinner."

Rachel stared at him, incredulous.

"I'm saved now, Rachel. By God's grace the sins are buried, forgiven. The burden is gone."

Rachel tried to focus her eyes on her husband, tried to comprehend him. She could feel Jerry's words dazing her, almost putting her in a trance. "Jerry," she said, her voice hardly there, "Jerry, you accepted Christ?"

"That's what I'm trying to tell you," he said, his eyes brilliant, jubilant as his voice. "That's what I'm saying, Rachel."

"I don't know what to say, Jerry. I prayed for you, I—"

"I know. You accomplished this with your prayers and your patience."

"I wasn't patient."

"No, don't say that. I made your life a nightmare, Rachel. I rejected you because in my twisted mind I thought you were rejecting me." His voice softened as he said, "But it will be all right now, Rae."

"What do you mean?"

"I want you to know, Rachel, I've broken off with Kit. Before—last summer—I was searching for something, for some meaning in my life, and I guess I thought Kit held that meaning. Or maybe I'm just using pretty words to excuse my sin, my selfishness, wanting something I had no right to. I don't know. But I was trying to fill a need in my life, an emptiness. Maybe I was really searching for an answer to my own guilt. The point is I know now that Christ is the only answer for a man—for me."

Rachel attempted to listen, trying to push the fuzziness out of her head. Who was this man? What did he have to do with her? For months she had tried to expel him from her life, from her emotions. She had nearly convinced herself that he was no part of her. She was a whole person, a woman, without him. But now, what he was saying at this moment, was important, vital, something she had to deal with. Why did she feel so numb? "I can't believe this is you talking, Jerry," she said, shaking her head.

He leaned forward. His face was flushed, his expression animated. He talked quickly. "For the first time I know where I'm going, Rachel, and I know why. I know why God put me here. I know that the world's problems are the result of sin, and there's an answer to sin. That's the beauty of it, the beauty of salvation. It's the one real answer. People spend all their lives looking for answers, and here it is. Here it is all the time! But you know all of this."

She smiled, not looking directly at him but only in

his direction. "I used to feel that kind of excitement, that enthusiasm, like you have now. I used to feel that way."

"What do you mean, *used to*?"

"I don't know, Jerry. I can't seem to hold on to that feeling anymore, the joy of being a Christian. I try and try—"

"You don't have to feel anything, Rachel. What do you have to feel?"

"I don't know," she said vaguely.

"Have I done this to you, driven you away from the Lord? Did I do this?"

"No, of course not, Jerry. It's just that everything has pulled me down. I seem to struggle with the Lord, trying to get closer to Him."

Jerry went to Rachel and sat by her. She moved slightly, neither accepting nor rejecting his closeness. He touched her face with his hands, gently touching, stroking. She sat immobile, saying nothing, her eyes directed away from him. Within her was the desire to rejoice with him, but she could not move, could not respond. What did he want from her? What did he want her to say? What was wrong, that she could not respond?

"Rachel," he said softly, "I want you back. I want to come home. I want us together again."

She said nothing; her eyes remained focused somewhere else, on some indefinite spot. Her thoughts were locked within her. She sat very still.

"Did you hear me, Rachel? I want us together again. Do you understand?"

"Yes, I hear you, I hear you," she said, her voice echoing mechanically. "I don't know what to say. I need time. I can't take all of this in at once. Can you understand? I'm happy for you, but I need time."

"Yes, yes, of course," Jerry said slowly. There was disappointment in his voice, disappointment etched into the lines of his face. He seemed perplexed, confused. "I won't push you, Rae. I won't push you," he said, vaguely reassuring her.

Rachel wasn't sure that she was listening.

Chapter Seventeen

Rachel was in no mood to go shopping but she allowed herself to be talked into it. Marlene was an excellent persuader. It was a warm Saturday morning. A clothing store was having a spring sale or pre-Easter sale or perhaps just an end-of-winter sale. Who knew? It was a sale.

Neatly lettered posterboard signs adorned the windows and the counters: Ladies Shirts and Sweaters, $6.87, Reg. $9.99. Bonded Acrylic Pant Suits $14.97. In the yardage department, signs glittered in slick, bright yellows and oranges: Hand Screened Orlon Challis Prints, $3.79 yd.; 100% Polyester Double Knits, $5.59 yd.

Marlene couldn't quite make up her mind whether she wanted to purchase a new dress or buy some material to make her own. Obligingly, Rachel followed her through the yardage department, chatting amiably as they inspected rolls and rolls of material.

Later, she browsed with Marlene through the endless racks of women's dresses, occasionally offering her opinion or randomly checking a price tag. However, tents and muumuus were not in style, and there was no possible way that Rachel could have squeezed herself into any of these delicate, clinging outfits. Marlene suggested loyally that they look in the maternity department, but Rachel waved her off, laughing, saying she wasn't going to spend $25 for a dress she could wear only another month or so.

"Well, I wouldn't be putting out any money for a dress right now either if it weren't such a special occasion," said Marlene eagerly, her fingers breezing through a rack of colorful garments.

Rachel smiled and said nothing, knowing Marlene wanted to tell her again what she had already told her three times this morning.

"He called and I didn't even know who it was at first," said Marlene breathlessly. "I thought maybe it was my boss calling to tell me he had to go out of town or something. I couldn't believe it was Mr. Timmons. I mean Stan. He said I should call him Stan, or Stanley, if I want. Some people call him Stan; some call him Stanley. Well, I mean, it doesn't matter—but there he was, Mr. Timmons—Stan—on the phone asking me to have dinner with him. Just like that. I couldn't believe it."

"Did he say how he happened to call?" asked Rachel. There was a chair nearby and she sat down, relieved to be off her feet for a moment.

"He just said he thought it was time for us to get a little better acquainted. You know how I've prayed about this."

"Yes, I do. It's an answer to prayer."

"It sure is," Marlene agreed happily. She removed a dress from the rack and inspected the price tag. "Of course," she added slyly, "that's not the only tremendous answer to prayer."

"What do you mean?"

"You know what I mean," said Marlene, deliberately avoiding Rachel's gaze, directing her attention instead to the garment in her hands. "Say, do you like this one?"

128

she asked. "It's a size 14. Bet I couldn't get into it though."

"It's pretty. Why don't you try it on? Now what did you mean?" Rachel insisted.

Marlene ignored her. "I've been gaining lately, I'm sure I have." She held the dress up and scrutinized her image in the mirror. "I bet I'm at least a 16 now," she said.

"Well, try it on and see."

Marlene hesitated, glancing shrewdly at Rachel. "What I meant before was that I think it's tremendous about Jerry being saved."

Rachel nodded. "Yes, it is."

"You don't sound exactly euphoric about it."

"I'm happy for him, Marlene. Of course I'm happy."

"Then what's the matter?"

Rachel shrugged. "He wants to come back home now."

"What's wrong with that?"

"Nothing, except—well, I don't know if I can change my feelings overnight, just like that. I mean, in my mind I know we should get back together, but I don't feel the same about him."

"You're still hurt."

"Well, sure I am. Why wouldn't I be? These last few months have been terrible. I didn't know it could be so bad."

"Then you do love Jerry?"

"I suppose I do. But, Marlene, it's not a fresh pure love anymore. It's all tarnished and marred. There are so many other things besides love mixed into my feelings now. I resent Jerry. I resent everything he's done to me. I know it's a sin, but that's how I feel."

"You know he's going to church now, don't you?"

"Yes, I saw him last Sunday. We didn't say much, but he asked me if I'd go out with him sometime."

"For a date?"

"Yeah, a date. Kind of funny, huh? Dating your own husband?"

"I'd say it's a good start. When are you going out?"

"The date? Next Friday night. I don't know what we'll do. But I know I should give him a chance, Marlene. I'm willing to let the Lord change my attitudes. I want you to know that."

"Good, I'm glad, Rachel," said Marlene, pleased. "When the two of you get back together, then the Lord will really be able to bless you. Now if you'll hold my purse for me, I'll go see if I can struggle into this luscious size 14."

They stopped for lunch at a nearby cafe and ordered tuna fish sandwiches and iced tea. Marlene had chocolate pie for dessert; Rachel had a small dish of vanilla ice cream. It was good to sit down, eat, talk and relax.

"I shouldn't eat this pie," mused Marlene, opening her mouth for another forkful. "That dress barely fit me as it is."

"Nonsense, it fit you perfectly." Rachel said, smiling.

Marlene returned a long, appraising look. "How do you feel, Rachel? You look kind of tired."

"I am. The least little thing I do makes me tired now. But I enjoyed today, I really did."

"That's fine, but I'm taking you right home, and I want you to get to bed and take a nap for the rest of the afternoon."

"We'll see," said Rachel reluctantly. "But I'm really all right. It's just that I've been having some false labor pains lately. They don't really hurt but they're annoying."

Marlene looked concerned. "False labor? What do you mean?"

Rachel put her hand on her stomach. "It's sort of a tightening, a hardness of the muscles right here. I remember feeling this way with Brian."

"Maybe you're going to have the baby soon, Rachel. You can't tell. I've never had a baby, but I had this aunt who had just the littlest backache and the next thing you know—"

"Marlene, believe me, the baby isn't due for five or six weeks yet. The doctor said this is normal; the muscles are just contracting to get in practice for the big day. Sort of like rehearsing, you know?"

They both laughed. "I'm just glad you're the one having the baby," said Marlene, scraping the last crumbs of pie from her plate.

"Well, I'm trying to get prepared. I even bought some books."

"Books?"

"Books on natural childbirth, things like that. I was scared to death when I had Brian. I didn't know anything. I want to be ready this time."

"What can a book tell you about having a baby?"

"Oh, there's a lot the mother can do to prepare herself—exercises and things."

"Exercises?"

"Sure. Have you ever head of 'psychoprophylaxis'?"

"Heard of it? I can't even say it."

Rachel laughed. "See, I'm trying to impress you with my knowledge. It means preparing a woman psychologically and physically for childbirth. It's called the Lamaze method, with breathing exercises and all."

"I can't imagine it," sighed Marlene.

"I may even sign up for a natural childbirth class," laughed Rachel.

"If it were me, I'd tell them to put me out until it's all over with. I wouldn't want to know a thing."

"I don't agree," said Rachel. "I can't stand to feel helpless, out of control. I don't want it to be like last time, being so scared, not knowing what's about to happen. I couldn't go through that again."

"Well, I admire your determination," said Marlene. She paused, then added reflectively, "You were so depressed for a while, but you look happier now."

"I am, Marlene. I really want this baby now. I can feel him moving around, and he's starting to seem real to me. You know, he even gets hiccups. Can you believe that?"

"You're kidding me."

"No, I'm not. Really, hiccups. I can actually feel them."

They both laughed again. For a change, it seemed quite natural and easy to laugh.

The phone was ringing when Rachel got home. She fumbled with her key and finally got the door open, but Brian was there and already had the phone. "It's for me," he said and turned his back to talk.

Rachel went into her bedroom and removed her dress and shoes and slipped into a bathrobe. Her feet were swollen and her legs ached. She definitely needed to rest, to take a nap. But she had better put out something to thaw for dinner, pork chops perhaps. Brian liked pork chops. She started for the kitchen where she could hear Brian still talking on the phone. She paused; there was something in Brian's voice that made her stop.

"I told you, nobody's going to find it," he said, his voice a rough whisper. "I got it taken care of, man. It's okay."

Brian's tone was menacing; he sounded frightened, angry. He didn't sound like himself at all. Rachel's skin felt prickly and cold.

When Brian got off the phone and came to her, his face was white and drawn. There was something behind his expression, a sort of cryptic message, which Rachel could not read. He smiled and the look vanished; he was just Brian.

He asked how she was feeling. He was solicitous, but he was in a hurry too. Was there anything he could do for her before going out? He had to go out. He had things to do. She wanted to know where he was going, how long he would be gone. To Ronnie's. They were working together on a school project—a biology assignment due Monday. He would be home early, as soon as possible. He brushed a kiss on her forehead and waved a hand in the air as he went out the door. Then, like that, he was gone.

Rachel lay down on her bed, exhausted, too tense to relax. She tried to sleep, but sleep was elusive now. Ideas, random thoughts, bombarded her mind, swirled in her head. Why couldn't she rest? What was wrong? Something about Brian bothered her. There was something in his expression that froze inside her, leaving her cold and afraid. When he had talked to her his voice was smooth as crystal, bright, flowing; but on the phone his voice had been sharp and jagged, like splintered glass.

Who was he talking to? Ronnie? Probably. What

were they saying? Something about hiding something—no, something about no one finding it—what? What would no one find? What was he hiding? Why would Brian hide something?

Brian is in trouble, thought Rachel. She sat up, startled. Trouble? Brian in trouble? She got up and went to his room, as if the calm order of his room might reassure her. Everything was in its place; everything was all right.

What would a young boy hide from people, from his parents, his mother? Rachel wondered. What would he feel the need to hide? A *Playboy* centerfold? Cigarettes? Things stolen from some store?

Brian's room was in order, nothing out of place. But perhaps something was hidden here, cached away; it must be here, whatever it was. Where else but here in Brian's room, his world, where he kept his treasures?

She could begin by searching; she could go through the whole room, turning things upside-down, until she found the secret, the thing that made Brian a puzzle to her now. If she chose, she could spend hours looking for clues to this boy she no longer understood.

Or could she? Rachel had always trusted Brian. His things belonged to him, were his private affair. She had never invaded that privacy; she had always respected his rights.

But there was something here.

No one will find it, he had said. She had heard him say it.

Rachel went to Brian's bureau and eased open a drawer. Each week she went to this bureau and opened the drawers, putting away clean clothes—socks, underwear, sweaters, shirts. She made neat orderly piles of Brian's clothing, smoothing out wrinkles, item after item in neat stacks. She knew these drawers and kept them in good order. There could be nothing here, nothing to suspect.

However, there was the bottom drawer—Brian's junk drawer, they called it—which she had no reason to keep in order, no reason to notice at all. It was full of the things Brian collected, odds and ends, she supposed. Once he had kept toy trucks and plastic soldiers and bits and pieces of broken games there, in that bottom drawer that was lowest and most accessible to a child. Now, who knew what was there?

She leaned down awkwardly and finally had to get on her knees to open the drawer. She would look here quickly and then that was it—Brian's secrets were his own. She would look nowhere else, but this one drawer just might offer a clue.

The drawer was a shambles, a vast disarray of random articles—stacks of baseball cards, string, old schoolwork, photographs of school friends, a rock collection from Big Bear, a tattered book of Jerry's on auto mechanics, a worn cigar box with—

She opened the box.

Cigarettes. She might have known, cigarettes.

No, no, not cigarettes. She looked closer, bringing the box up to her face. She picked up one long taper, very narrow, thin, and turned it between her fingers. The paper was odd, twisted at the ends. The smell—

Somehow she knew.

"Oh, God, no," she said, "not marijuana, not marijuana."

She sat on the floor and began to sob. "Dear God, please not Brian," she cried. "Please, please, not Brian, not my son, not Brian!"

Chapter Eighteen

The doorbell rang. Rachel was there immediately, opening the door before the echo of ringing had faded, welcoming Jerry into the room, greeting him formally without a smile. She observed at once the cords of strain in his face. Reading his eyes, she knew that he sensed the same painful tension in her.

"Jerry," she said, but her thoughts trailed off like wind.

"Rachel, I'm glad you called me," he said briskly, rubbing his hands together as if they might be numb with cold, although it was not cold outside. "You were right to call," he said again in his business voice.

"I didn't know what else to do," she replied, hardly more than whispering.

"Brian's smoking pot—that's how it looks?"

"I don't know. I think so. I found marijuana in his room, in a cigar box in his drawer. I'm sure it's marijuana."

"Where is it?"

"There." She indicated a box on the coffee table.

Jerry inspected the box, examining the contents painstakingly. The severity of his expression silenced Rachel, although she had a dozen questions to ask him. She waited for him to finish his investigation and turn again to her, and when at last he did, there was a brittleness to his voice. "I was afraid of this—I should have realized—"

"What are we going to do? Brian will be home any time."

"I suppose we should turn this stuff over to the police."

"The police? Turn our own son over to the police? Jerry, no!"

"I didn't say that; I don't mean—"

Rachel sat down, curving her body into the contour of the couch. Beckoning Jerry to sit down, she curled herself awkwardly into one corner, making room for him. He dropped down beside her heavily. From the blankness of his face, Rachel had the impression that his mental acuity had been short-circuited. This disturbed her. She needed something from him—strength, good advice, a solution.

"Brian's only 13," she said thickly, feeling a vague growing panic inside. "Just a child, Jerry. We've got to help him. We have to do something to help him out of this."

Jerry managed to shake his mind free finally and looked at her imploringly. The tendons in his neck were taut, bulging slightly beneath the skin. "I don't know what to do," he said.

"I don't either."

"I noticed little things about Brian," he said, "but I tried to tell myself they didn't mean anything. What about you, Rachel? Have you noticed signs, any indications that Brian is on drugs?"

Rachel shrugged apologetically. "Just the things you already know about—his school grades slipping, things like that," she replied unevenly. "He was gone a lot, you know that. He wouldn't confide in me."

"Did you notice any erratic behavior, mental confusion, extreme moods?"

Rachel shook her head. "I don't think so, Jerry." Her voice was too loud, thin and sharp like steel, like a knife. "I don't think so!"

"Can't you be sure?" he demanded.

"No, no, I can't. I can't think right now. I'm too upset to remember anything."

Jerry pushed the bulk of his frame back into the couch and sighed deeply. Reaching out, he took her hand and gently rubbed his thumb over her delicate fingers. "I'm sorry, Rae. I didn't mean to start in on you," he said softly. "I'm as upset as you are. This thing leaves me cold. I just don't know what to do."

Rachel nodded shakily. She was aware that Jerry's breathing was labored; he seemed to be fighting to control some secret outrage within himself. She could feel its power surging from his hand into hers, through her. There was a certain strength, a rawbone courage, in such anger.

With her free hand she touched his arm, his wrist, drew her fingers lightly up along the length of his forearm, aware of the fine layer of hair on the back of his arm and the tanned flesh and solid bone of his wrist. Her touch would be only brief comfort for this tired man, but at least a spontaneous gesture of—what? Affection? Love?

She attempted a smile. "We'll think of something, Jerry, something. Can I get you some coffee?"

"No, no thanks, Rachel—unless you want some. Have you eaten yet?"

"No, I was going to fix pork chops for dinner, but I got sidetracked. I'm not hungry now."

"You should eat. Something light, a snack. How about some scrambled eggs? I'll join you—"

She hesitated only a moment, then nodded.

They went to the kitchen and Jerry sat down at the table while Rachel put a frying pan on the stove, melted some butter, broke eggs into the sizzling yellow fat, and stirred the mixture vigorously with a fork until the liquid thickened into fluffy golden mounds.

"It helps to be doing something," Rachel said, taking plates from the cupboard. She served the eggs and poured two glasses of milk and sat down beside Jerry.

"Looks great," he said.

"Thanks. I feel better keeping busy, not quite so strung out."

"Good."

"Before you arrived, Jerry, I was trying to think what I know about drugs, and, you know, I really couldn't think of much. I've read magazine articles, newspaper stories, and even seen a few TV specials, but outside of that, what do I know? What do I know about real people needing drugs or playing around with narcotics? It doesn't make any sense to me, Jerry. I can't relate to it. So how can I talk to Brian?"

"I don't know, Rachel."

"I keep saying there has to be a logical explanation for this, something to explain it away so it will be as if I never found that cigar box, as if there were nothing to find."

"It's not like that," replied Jerry. "It did happen. Something's going on and we have to find out what it is."

"Will he tell us?"

"I hope so, Rachel. I sure hope so."

While they talked, they ate eagerly, as if they had underestimated their hunger. When Jerry finished his eggs, he sat back and looked thoughtfully at his wife. "You know, Rachel," he said, "a person tries to be fairly so-phisticated about life, mature, all of that. But when it comes right down to it, when something hits you where you live, all of your objectivity goes right out the win-dow—and you're just as vulnerable, just as open to hurt as the next guy."

"You really feel that way?" Rachel asked, vaguely surprised. "I hadn't thought of you being hurt; hurt im-plies being weak, soft—"

"It implies caring," corrected Jerry.

Rachel nodded. "Yes, yes, you're right, of course."

"But I also feel guilty, Rachel."

"Guilty? Why?"

"I fought you and Brian so much. I rejected your faith, ridiculed you."

"It wasn't just you, Jerry. It was everything. Me, Brian, the whole situation. We all contributed. And you weren't a Christian; you didn't realize—"

"That's no excuse."

"No, but I feel guilty too."

"You? What did you do?"

Rachel toyed with her fork, tracing the flower design on her Melmac plate. "I don't know if I can explain, Jerry. It's just that I haven't let the Lord have control of me for a long time. I know there's so much the Lord would open up for me, if I'd let Him. But for months I've been wrapped up in my own little world of resent-ment and bitterness. I admit, Jerry, I've been bitter to-ward you, but I don't want to be anymore. I'm sorry. I thought I was struggling with the Lord to get closer to Him, but now I think I was just trying to have the good feeling that comes from His closeness without submit-ting to His will. Does that make sense?"

"I think so. I'm just learning, but I think I can understand that."

"I don't want it to be that way anymore. I want God to forgive the resentment and take it away. But I think I've already hurt Brian, and what scares me is that although God forgives sin, He doesn't always take away the consequences of sin. That's what worries me now."

"God is fair, Rachel. We have to trust Him. The only thing I know to do is to trust Him with this."

"Yes," agreed Rachel. She got up from the table and cleared away the plates and glasses. Jerry helped her rinse the dishes and stack them on the counter. They started for the living room but stopped suddenly when they heard the click of the front door. Brian came in, hurrying, his feet moving in quick smooth strides across the carpet. He was whistling something, a familiar popular tune.

"Brian," said Jerry curtly.

The boy turned abruptly, obviously startled, and stared at them. "What's going on?" he said, smiling unevenly, sounding breathless. "Dad, what are you doing here?"

Chapter Nineteen

Brian stared quizzically at his dad. "How come you're here tonight?" he asked.

Before Jerry could answer, Brian's gaze drifted across the room and picked up the cigar box on the table. He shot a comprehending glance at his parents and stormed: "What are you doing getting into my stuff? Who said you could snoop into my things? That's private property, that stuff; it's none of your business!"

"It's my business if you're smoking marijuana," replied Jerry sharply.

"Marijuana? Where'd you get a crazy idea like that?"

"From that box," Jerry answered.

Brian stiffened, throwing back his lean, angular shoulders. "That stuff isn't mine. You should have left it alone. It doesn't belong to me."

"Then whose is it?" asked Rachel.

"Nobody's. I can't say."

"Ronnie Mayhew's?"

"No."

"Then whose?"

"Nobody's."

"Brian," cried Rachel, going to the boy, touching his face. "Talk to us, please. Tell us about it. We have to know."

He brushed her hand away. "There's nothing to tell.

143

Nothing."

Jerry jumped forward and grabbed his son's arm. "Don't act like that with your mother," he said sternly. "Don't you dare act like that with her."

Brian relented. "I'm sorry," he muttered, shaking himself free.

"We just want to help you, Brian," Rachel said quietly. "Please let us help."

"I don't need help. What are you ganging up on me for? I didn't do anything."

"We found marijuana in your room, Brian. That's something; that's plenty," Jerry insisted caustically.

Rachel interrupted. "Can't we just sit down and talk about this calmly?"

"All right. Let's sit down, Brian."

"What for?"

"So we can talk, you, your mother, and I."

"There's nothing to talk about."

"I want to know if you're taking drugs!" Jerry shouted.

"What difference does it make?"

"Are you kidding me? What's wrong with your head, boy?"

"Jerry, please," Rachel pleaded. "If we all get angry, we won't get anywhere."

Jerry looked at Rachel. The hard knot of anger in his expression loosened and fell away. "I'm sorry," he said. Without anger in his face he looked tired and drained; there was a slackening of his jowls, a sort of sagging weariness around the jaw that gave Rachel a fleeting impression of an old man. He sat down and rubbed his hands over his temples. Rachel and Brian sat down.

"We have to get this thing worked out," insisted

Jerry. "This is serious, Brian. Can't you see that this is a serious matter?"

"It's no big deal."

"Suppose you let your mother and me decide that, okay?"

"I guess," he said grudgingly.

"Now what's the story, Brian?"

"Nothing. I was just doing a guy a favor."

"What do you mean?"

"This guy thought his old lady—his mother—was getting wise to him, so he asked if I'd stash the grass at my place for a while."

"And you thought that was perfectly all right to do?" asked Jerry skeptically.

"Why not? I didn't smoke the joints, Dad. I was just helping him out for a few days."

"Do you expect me to believe that?"

"Believe what you want."

"I don't want any smart talk from you, Brian. I don't know what's gotten into you lately. I don't even know you anymore."

"Can I go now?"

"Go? Go where?"

"To my room."

"You'll go to your room when I'm through with you, not before," Jerry snapped.

"Brian," said Rachel tentatively, "would you just tell us who gave you the marijuana?"

"I can't."

"Why not?"

"I promised him I wouldn't."

"But whoever he is, he needs help, Brian. Surely you can see that."

Brian's mouth snapped rigid; he stared at the floor, silent. He sat hunched forward, his arms locked around his knees, his manner imperturbably stoical, subtly defiant. Finally he said, "I don't want to talk anymore, Mother. Please let me go to my room. I feel sick."

"You stay where you are until we settle this," Jerry said angrily.

"But I think I'm going to throw up."

"Jerry, please—"

"All right, Rachel, all right," Jerry conceded reluctantly. "But listen to me, Brian. You are not to go out of this house for a month. You go to school and come home, that's it. No friends, no social activities, nothing. Do you understand?"

"Yes."

"And, Brian, I'm going to call the pastor and find out if he'll see the three of us tomorrow after church. We need help, Brian. All three of us."

It seemed to Rachel that Brian pulled himself to his feet like a wobbly marionette whose arms and legs might at any moment spring crazily in all directions. Outwardly, Brian was not so undone, but Rachel sensed that he might be flying apart inside, too stubborn to admit he needed help.

"Can I go to my room now, Dad?" he asked evenly.

"Yes, go on."

When Brian had shut the door to his room, Jerry looked at Rachel and muttered, "I guess it's time for me to go, too."

Rachel nodded wordlessly, watching him. He went to the door, but stood there, apparently reluctant to leave. He cracked his knuckles nervously.

Rachel went to him, facing him, unsure of what to

say. What could either of them say? She had the feeling that, were she to encourage him, Jerry might impulsively gather her into his arms; he might kiss her suddenly and tell her he wanted to stay. She almost welcomed his closeness, his touch. Almost. But that was not something for her to think about now.

"I'm sorry it went like this," Jerry said softly. "I had hoped we could clear this up. I hoped Brian would be cooperative."

"What can we do now?"

"We'll talk with Dr. Emrick. Maybe he can reach Brian."

"Isn't there anything else we can do?"

"Pray, of course. I'm also considering contacting Mr. Mayhew, Ronnie's father, to see if he knows anything about all of this."

"Then you do think Brian is protecting Ronnie Mayhew?"

"Who else?"

"You'll let me know if you find out anything?"

"Yes, I will."

"Thank you. Good night, Jerry."

"Good night, Rae. I'll see you tomorrow after church—with Brian. And don't forget our date next Friday night."

"I won't," she said, smiling.

"I'm counting on that," he said as he went out, closing the door gently between them.

Chapter Twenty

Rachel felt a certain anticipation about this evening, a vague expectancy that she could not define or understand. It was a feeling that made her just a little breathless. Glancing at Jerry beside her in the car, she said, "It's really a perfect evening, isn't it?"

He laughed lightly. "Yes, it is. Can you believe April is here already?"

"No," said Rachel. "Where does the time go?"

"I don't know," he replied, "but I want to tell you that you look beautiful tonight. I want time to stand still so I can look at you."

"Thank you," said Rachel, actually blushing a little. "Am I allowed to know where we're going or is it a surprise?"

He shot her a quick, knowing glance, grinning boyishly, then turned his attention back to the traffic.

Jerry's Mustang propelled them onto the Long Beach Freeway, lurching them into the outside lane where they joined the slow-moving queues of early evening traffic. The sky was bathed in pastel-shaded dusk—oranges and yellows, a melting sherbet mixture, with the sun a solid scooped ball of cinnamon hovering precariously close to the earth. It was lovely, this time of evening, this sudden final blush of color on the horizon before night surged over everything, blotting out the landscape in a single sweep, pervasive and complete.

"I asked if tonight is a surprise," insisted Rachel when she received no answer.

"A surprise?" mused Jerry, gently mocking. "A surprise? Well, that depends. Are you in the mood for barbecued sweet and sour spareribs, won ton soup, pork chow mein and the lightest almond cookies in the whole Los Angeles area?"

"And miniature china teapots of clear, very hot tea?" said Rachel brightly, catching his enthusiasm. "And chopsticks that we can't possibly eat with?"

"You bet."

"Sounds wonderful to me."

"Great. There's this little place not far from here. It doesn't look too impressive from the outside, but it's quiet and the atmosphere is pleasant. I thought you'd like that better than a place with crowds and dazzling lights and jangling music."

"It sounds perfect, Jerry."

"And after a leisurely meal, I thought we'd drive into Los Angeles to the Music Center. I have tickets for a concert at the Dorothy Chandler Pavilion. How does that itinerary sound?"

"I'd like that, Jerry. The Music Center is beautiful. We were there once before, and it was lovely."

"I remembered that you liked it. It won't be too tiring for you, will it?"

"I don't think so. Sometimes it bothers me now to sit for very long at a time, but if the baby acts up, perhaps we could leave during an intermission—but I don't expect any problems," Rachel assured him quickly.

"Good. Just let me know. We don't want to take any chances with that little guy."

"Or girl," said Rachel with a smile.

"Yeah. Or girl," Jerry grinned. His expression changed slightly, and he asked, "How has Brian been this past week?"

Rachel thought a moment. "Quiet, I would say. He keeps to himself."

"Then you don't think Dr. Emrick's talk had any effect on him?"

"I don't know. In a way, he seems obedient. He comes right home from school and does his homework. He's very polite. As far as I know he hasn't seen any of his friends, not even Ronnie, except perhaps at school."

"Good. That's a start. I just hope it's not too late, Rachel. The talk you and I had with Dr. Emrick was a real eye-opener for me."

"What do you mean?"

"Well, he made me realize that even though our salvation is secure, we still have a fight on our hands. I didn't see that clearly until our talk with Dr. Emrick on Sunday. What I mean is, I still have a lot to learn about God, about who He is and what my responsibility to Him involves. I have this feeling, Rachel, that it would be awfully easy for me to think of God as being created for me rather than me being created for Him."

"That's a strange thing to say," said Rachel candidly.

"I know," admitted Jerry, "but it's something I'm convicted about. I find myself thinking that God can do this for me and He can do that and if only He would make this happen—you know, a job, things settled with Brian, our problems solved—"

"I do that too, Jerry. I get terribly perturbed or impatient if God doesn't work something out the way I think it should be."

Jerry nodded but kept his eyes on the road.

"Our problem is that we see ourselves at the center of things, with God at the periphery. We think of God in terms of what He can do for us to make us happier or to answer our prayers or to give us good feelings."

"There's nothing wrong with those things."

"No, but it's like Dr. Emrick pointed out. A Christian should be aware that the God of the universe is at the core of all things, the absolute center, and we are created for Him, to glorify Him. When our lives are truly God-centered, *Christ-centered*, then the other things fall into place." Jerry glanced at Rachel and smiled. "Then there's this matter of obedience, Rachel. How do we really obey God? Do you ever think about that?"

"Yes, I've considered it a great deal since our talk with Dr. Emrick. And Jerry, I feel closer to the Lord now than I've felt in a long time."

"How do you explain that?"

"Well, for one thing, I've been reading my Bible and praying. But that's not the whole answer because I was trying to do that, at times, before. The difference is that now I've yielded inside. It sure is good to feel like I'm back in touch with God again."

"That's good, Rachel. Then you haven't let Brian's problem tear you down."

"No," Rachel replied. "Sometimes a wave of panic will go through me for an instant, but this peace I have goes deeper."

For a moment, Jerry was silent. While he lightly thumped his fingers on the steering wheel, his expression grew cloudy, curiously opaque. There was almost a haggard quality to the set of his jaw.

"Is anything wrong?" ventured Rachel.

"Not really," Jerry replied. "It's just that after talking with Dr. Emrick, I realize I really blew it that night with Brian. I lost my cool and exploded, and Brian naturally retaliated. It works on me—the fact that I failed. I know it's going to take a lot of wisdom to deal with Brian, and I don't know if I can handle it."

"We seem to have such a long way to go with him," Rachel said.

"Yes, and it's not just Brian's problem either. It's all three of us. I hope a few more sessions with Dr. Emrick will help straighten things out. You and I have things to settle between us, Rachel, and we have things to settle with Brian."

"Yes, I know," Rachel admitted. "It hurts to think that Brian may be turning to drugs now because he is lacking something from his home life, something we should have been giving him."

"It's hard to accept," Jerry agreed. "When Dr. Emrick first suggested that we needed treatment along with Brian, my first impulse was to punch him in the nose. Stupid, huh? I mean, this feeling just broke inside me, this angry, overwhelming frustration. It tore me up inside to think I had failed at something as important as raising my own son."

"I know, Jerry. That's why it was so important to me to get things straightened out with the Lord. I think I can approach this problem with Brian now without feeling so guilty and defeated."

"I think we'll make it all right, Rachel," he said confidently, hitting the turn signal for the next freeway off-ramp. They wound off onto a surface road and made a left turn. There was no longer any hint of color in the sky overhead, but the darkness was broken into pieces at the horizon by innumerable distant city lights—street lamps, freeway beacons, flashing neon signs, window-lights gleaming from great, jutting high-rise buildings, and the strung-out glitter of shopping centers.

"By the way, did you contact Ronnie Mayhew's father?" asked Rachel, thinking still of Brian.

"Yes. I went to see him at his work. He has quite an impressive office; he's a vice president or general manager or something, I can't remember."

"You didn't accuse Ronnie of anything, did you?"

"No, of course not. I just told Mr. Mayhew about the situation with Brian and suggested the possibility that Ronnie could be involved."

"What did he say?"

"He blew up at me, nearly threw me out of his office. He said just because I was having problems with my boy, I had no right to try to get his son in trouble."

"Did he really say that?"

"He said his son has everything a boy could want and has no reason to fool around with drugs."

"Then you didn't get anywhere with him?"

"Nowhere."

"I'm sorry, Jerry. I felt sure Ronnie was involved."

"I'm sure he is."

A thoughtful silence fell between the two of them until, in a little Los Angeles suburb that Rachel didn't recognize, Jerry swung the Mustang into a narrow driveway separating a brick building from a busy Taco Bell stand with signs advertising two tacos for the price of one and free balloons for the kiddies. Rachel watched as people worked their way through ragged lines toward a window to receive cardboard boxes of food in orange wrappers. Children, milling about, tore off the wrappers and devoured tacos or enchiladas. There was a carnival hysteria about the place that both attracted and irritated Rachel; she watched until Jerry brought the car to a stop behind the brick building. This place stood in sharp contrast to the circus atmosphere nearby. Having few windows and a narrow, inconspicuous door, the structure seemed totally impervious to the world, a blockade, a bastion, cryptic and hushed as a tomb.

Jerry smiled feebly and said, "It doesn't look like much from the outside, but the food is great."

"I think it looks—extraordinary," said Rachel, laughing, feeling within herself a sudden, rising, gusty pleasure from the presence of this man, her husband—a stranger who was perhaps becoming her friend.

Chapter Twenty-One

It was nearly 11 when Rachel and Jerry left the pavilion. They took their time walking to the car, entranced, the music they had heard still swirling in their heads. The air smelled especially clean tonight. It seemed to touch them with magic, invigorating them. When they reached the Mustang, Jerry, helping Rachel into the car, asked, "Are you tired, Honey?"

"Not very," she said, smiling.

"I want to talk to you about something," he told her seriously. "I thought perhaps we could take a drive along the ocean."

"All right."

"You're not too tired?"

"No, I'm fine, really."

"Did you enjoy the concert?"

"Yes, it was lovely. And the dinner was perfect too. I don't know when I've had such a nice evening, Jerry."

"I'm glad you had a good time. I did too. It's sort of like old times."

"Yes," she murmured wistfully.

They took the Harbor Freeway out of Los Angeles and later drove down Ocean Boulevard to Belmont Shore, where they found a narrow stretch of beach accessible from the road. Jerry pulled over to the side and turned off the ignition.

"How's this?" he said, shifting in the seat so that he faced Rachel.

"I love the view—what I can see; but it seems kind of funny being here. I mean, parking like this at the beach, like teenagers or something."

"I could have taken you home, but Brian would be there, and I wanted our talk to be private—just us."

"All right, Jerry."

"Say, what did you do with those little fortune cookies? Where are they?"

Rachel laughed, a little embarrassed. "They're in my purse." She pulled out a napkin and spread it open on what was left of her lap. "You're laughing at me," she said, amiably accusing him. "You think I'm silly to save these, but I'll bet you're hungry now, aren't you?"

"All right, I'm game. Give me a fortune cookie."

"See, I told you. Wait, Jerry, you have to read what it says—the little paper inside. Don't eat the paper."

Chuckling, Jerry broke open the cookie, removed the narrow strip of paper and held it up to the window where enough street light penetrated the glass to bring the words on the paper into focus. "Do something nice for someone near."

"What?"

"You heard me—my fortune, compliments of Hong Kong."

"Here's mine. Can you read it?"

He held the narrow slip up to the light and read, "You will make friends with a stranger."

"A stranger? Wonderful. Who?"

"Me. How about me?"

She laughed lightly. "You're not a stranger."

"But I am. We're all strangers, Rachel. That's what we've been, a family of strangers."

"Now you're getting serious," she warned softly. "These cookies are a joke, Jerry, something to laugh at.

156

They don't mean anything."

"I'm not talking about fortune cookies anymore, Rachel. I'm talking about us, you and me. We have to talk and face things and make definite decisions."

"I know, Jerry, but—"

"Rachel, listen to me, listen."

"I am."

"I've been offered a good job with an engineering firm in Cleveland, Ohio, and I think I should accept it."

"Cleveland?"

"I can't keep collecting unemployment compensation week after week, and there just aren't that many good jobs available here right now. I've had my application in all over the place, including a few places back East, and this is the only promising thing to turn up. I've looked into the offer, and I feel I should take it."

"What am I supposed to say?"

"I hope you'll say you'll go with me. My parents don't live too far from Cleveland; it would be good for Brian—"

"Move to Ohio? You mean now, right away?"

"Soon. If I accept, they'll give me until June so Brian can finish out the school term."

"I can't give you any answer right away, Jerry. I just don't know. I don't know what to think."

"All right, Rachel," he said soberly. He was still holding pieces of the fortune cookie. Lifting them up ceremoniously in the palm of his hand, he said, "Here's to your silly little cookies, Rae. 'Do something nice for someone near.' I can do that." He leaned over and kissed Rachel lightly on the lips. She did not move or look at him. She simply wound her fortune cookie into her napkin, twisting the edges of the napkin tightly into white ragged snakes.

Jerry removed the napkin from her hands and let it fall to the floor, swallowed by darkness. Gently he took Rachel into his arms and kissed her, touching his lips to her forehead and eyes, to her lashes, moving his mouth over her ear to the softness of her hair. He held her head against his shoulder and caressed the back of her neck until she pulled away from him.

"Jerry—"

"No, no, Rachel."

"Jerry, please, I'm uncomfortable. I have to sit back."

"Are you all right?"

"Yes, but I'm tired, I—"

"Rachel, listen to me. You're my wife. I want you to be my wife. In a few weeks you're going to have my child. That baby needs us together; Brian needs us together. What do I have to say to get through to you?"

Rachel was silent. He kissed her again, a hard, demanding kiss that hurt her mouth. Rachel recognized within herself a wish to respond. But the desire inside her could not focus itself on anything specific; it was too vague, unsettled, fleeting like air, like the moist sea air seeping into the automobile. She wanted to feel intensely, to be sure of her feelings, to wash away the sediment of bitterness and erase the scars. How did one erase scars? Oh, God, what could she do?

Then, she was aware of something. This man—her husband—who sat close beside her, his breathing strained, his breath pungent but sweet, put his hands over his face and wept. His voice was muffled, breaking over waves of deep sweeping emotion. "I'm sorry, Rachel. I don't know what else to do. I love you, but I can't reach you. Should I leave you alone? Go away? What?"

"I—I don't know. I want to love you again, I want to. Help me—"

He kissed her again, slowly, with an astounding tenderness born out of anguish and desire. "Let yourself respond," he murmured against her lips. "Love me, Darling."

And Rachel, loosing the reins, opening her mind and heart, and releasing the bonds of bitterness that shackled her emotions, recognized that familiar swell of joy, of love, of acceptance and forgiveness, and returned her husband's kiss.

When Jerry released her, he was laughing, breathless, gleeful. "I want to run on the beach and shout our love to the stars," he said.

"We could paint it across the sky in huge, brilliant letters," cried Rachel.

"Yes. Come, darling, run in the sand with me. What do you say?"

"You're crazy, out of your mind," she laughed. "I'm as big as an elephant. I'd fall right down. I couldn't move—"

"No, I'll help you. I'll keep my arms around you."

"All right, yes. You can hold my hand all the way."

"We'll do everything—sing and cry and love—"

"I do love you, Jerry; I do."

"Rae, I love you more than I ever dreamed it was possible to love a woman. It's as if my love for God has made my love for you so much greater."

Rachel's voice was light, joyous. "Jerry, do you know, for the first time in my life I feel I can love you freely. We are one in Christ; that's just beginning to mean something to me. When I thought you didn't love me, I couldn't even let the fact that you were saved break down my barrier against you. I couldn't open myself to more hurt."

"But all along I said I wanted you back, Darling. I wanted to come home."

"But you didn't say you loved me. You never said that."

"But I do. I love you. You know I do."

"Yes, now, tonight, I know it. I know you love me."

He took her hand and gently kissed her fingers. "Do we walk on the beach or go home?" he asked softly.

"Go home."

"All right. But you understand, Rachel, tonight we go home together."

She pressed his hand against her cheek, delighting in its warmth. "Yes, that's good," she whispered. "I want you home."

It was well past midnight when Jerry unlocked the door for Rachel and flicked the light switch in the hallway. Arm in arm, they ambled in together with a certain conspiratorial air, a sweet sense of abandonment, as if they were incredibly young lovers meeting for a romantic tryst. Gently helping her with her coat, he kissed the back of her neck. Happily, dreamily, she kicked off her shoes and flung her purse on a chair and went to him for a caress.

"Should we wake Brian and tell him?" she whispered.

"No, let's tell him in the morning," Jerry murmured against the soft curls brushing her cheek. "Besides, he'll know when he sees me here."

"He'll be so surprised—"

The telephone rang, jangling their splendid mood into nothingness. Rachel stared at the phone as if waking from a dream. "Who . . . it's so late . . . who could be—"

"Probably a wrong number. I'll get it," said Jerry.

"Before it wakes Brian!"

Jerry grappled with the phone and barked huskily into the receiver. "Hello? Yes? Yes."

Watching, waiting, Rachel shifted her weight from one stockinged foot to the other and absently patted her hair into place, listening.

"Mrs. Webber?" said Jerry, sounding puzzled. "Yes, she's here. Who's calling please? What? Well, this is Mr. Webber, Brian's father. I don't understand. There must be some mistake. No, my son is here, asleep in his room. Just a moment." He turned to Rachel, motioning something.

"Brian? Is it about Brian?" she asked.

"Check his room," Jerry whispered, a clipped unmistakable urgency in his tone. He spoke into the phone again. "We're checking right now."

Rachel moved as swiftly as she could, but her steps were sluggish, as if she were swaying in slow motion, getting nowhere, struggling against dark waves of an imaginary sea. Her return from Brian's room was worse, a nightmare. "He's not there, Jerry. He's not in his room; he's gone!"

Jerry went white, his face stiffening. He put his mouth to the receiver. "Hello? Yes, that's right. We'll be right over. Do whatever is necessary. We're on our way."

Rachel listened without comprehension. "What is it, Jerry? What happened?"

There was a grisly, spangled vision in back of his eyes as he cried, "It's Brian. They've got him over at Long Beach Community Hospital. He took an overdose of drugs!"

161

Chapter Twenty-Two

The drive to the hospital was insufferably long, a ghastly trip constantly interrupted by hideous traffic lights that slammed the Mustang to a stop again and again. An irony, so many stop lights, when all along the streets were empty of traffic. So why the demanding lights, forcing Jerry to wait long precious moments for nothing in the empty streets?

Rachel clasped her hands and stared through the windshield, aware only of muted car sounds grinding a million miles away. One thought gripped her: *Brian, Brian, Brian. What about Brian?*

She ground her fingernails into her palm. Was she trembling? She was numb, suspended somehow, her senses revolving around that one focal point. Brian.

They were approaching the hospital now. Rachel stared ahead, stunned by the reality of buildings and grounds, sturdy, blank structures that held a secret. She would have to pry that secret out of those silent walls; the secret was Brian. Brian—a mystery, a puzzle, an unknown factor.

The hospital was an ordinary building, familiar, really. Made of stucco, a buff color. Old. Spanish architecture or something similar, with a sort of cloistered patio area at the entrance. It stood on a slight hill. The street in front of the hospital was narrow, making it difficult to pass cars or to circumvent automobiles parked at the curb. Brian was born in this hospital, so certainly it was familiar, a dusty forgotten familiarity.

Rachel had been here to tea just two weeks ago. One of those teas for prospective mothers, providing them with an opportunity to preregister so that they could check into the hospital later without the usual red tape. Rachel remembered that afternoon. A convivial coffee klatsch, during which a score of chattering, excited, very pregnant women were given a token tour of the maternity ward and then subjected to a flowery speech by some middle-aged woman—who may or may not have had children—on the joys of motherhood. Rachel had spent this time making out a shopping list.

Rachel's thoughts were sliced in two by the rumbling of Jerry's car as he pulled into the parking lot. The parking lot was an interminable distance from the hospital itself. Rachel's head ached with a pounding that was like words, beating over and over, saying something. It seemed to Rachel that she was on the verge of realizing some vital truth, something about Brian that would make him real to her, no longer a mystery; but the idea remained fuzzy in her mind and never actually assumed a particular shape. In fact, nothing was in focus. Everything blurred as if shot with rain.

Although the headache remained, Rachel's mind turned blank. Her body seemed empty. Yet it was heavy and dragged her down, and the child within her twisted and turned periodically, reminding her of its presence. This movement within her was more real than the actual outward movements involved in climbing out of the car and striding wearily toward the hospital door.

This was like a dream, composed of scattered fragments of reality. How could this be real? Only one thing was real: the mystery of Brian. Was he alive or dead? What terrible thing had happened that strangers should call for her in the middle of the night? What hideous sequence of events had led up to the horror of this moment?

What about Brian? What was he doing when she saw him last? What was he wearing? Tennis shoes, his blue striped shirt? No, the brown one; the blue one was missing a button. He had said, "I need this shirt fixed for school on Monday; the button's gone." He was reading a book at the time, history or geography or something, something about Mesopotamia. The dawn of civilization. He told her he would spend this evening writing a report. He would put a TV dinner in the oven; he would be fine. She should have a good time; say hello to Dad.

There was a great gap between that moment of pleasant ordinary conversation, and this present moment of frenzy. What had happened between? Dear God, what?

Inside the hospital was a hushed atmosphere, a strict, ritualistic observance of silence. The foyer was empty; the corridor seemed empty except for an occasional phantom shadow of a nurse or an orderly slipping in or out of a room. Even these few actions, performed anonymously by people in anonymous white outfits, seemed accomplished without sounds, no footsteps, no rustling of clothing, no hum of conversation. Rachel's own breathing was louder and more demanding than the accumulated sounds of this building.

They were in the foyer. Jerry was gripping her arm, holding too tightly, trying to steer her somewhere. The foyer, with muted overhead lights, was pleasantly dim.

Partitions and offices were to the left. Beside the information desk, artificial plants stood in plastic containers that looked like something more expensive—wood or stone, not plastic. The plants were too green and shiny—mere imitations.

Rachel stared toward the information desk. Someone was there, a white-haired woman with a bland face, thinly-penciled brows, and tidy, precise lips. She was writing something down, filling in blank spaces, very neat and exact.

Jerry went straight to the desk, gave his name and started to ask questions. Where was Brian? How was he? What had happened?

The woman smiled kindly and handed Jerry some official forms. "These should be signed before any underage person is admitted to the hospital. If you would take care of that now—"

Brian. What about Brian? Her answers were as neat and exact as her handwriting: Brian was in the emergency room. Dr. Whalen, the resident physician, was in attendance. Everything was being done. No, there were no details. Rachel and Jerry were welcome to wait in the foyer for someone to come and talk to them, to explain. She would let Emergency know that they were there. Someone would come shortly.

Reluctantly, Jerry and Rachel moved back toward the lobby and sat down on one of the sleek green vinyl couches. Ash trays and wire magazine racks and polished tables mixed in among the couches and chairs. Rachel stared at the walls and the corridor shooting off to nowhere. The walls seemed transparent and tediously repetitious. It was as if Rachel could see all the rooms and halls, an incredible labyrinth. She could imagine the labyrinth composed of endless cubicles housing flesh and blood bodies, all sick or impaired, all needing attention.

Rachel could smell the sickness, although it was masked by other smells of products used to clean away the odors of the flesh, of weakness, and of death. Chlorine, disinfectants, soaps. Rachel could smell them all. They absorbed the air and changed it.

This place was not like the rest of the world. It was not natural. Too much was covered up; illness was a business here, tidy, orderly, a matter of computerized cards and signatures on dotted lines.

What was she doing here? Waiting for Brian? It was a lie. Brian wasn't here. There was nothing here of Brian.

"What are you thinking about?"

"What? What did you say?"

"Your expression—what are you thinking of?" asked Jerry.

"Nothing. Brian. Where is he? What's happening?"

"I don't know."

"They should let us go to him. How can they keep us away? How?"

"They're doing it, Darling."

"But why?"

"We have to wait."

"We must do something, Jerry. We can't just sit here."

"Do you want me to call the pastor?" he asked.

"Dr. Emrick? No. What can he do? It's the middle of the night."

"I just thought—"

"No, let him sleep. Wait till we find out something.

Maybe Brian's all right. Maybe we can take him home."

"I pray to God—!"

Suddenly there was a sound, the banging of a door. A man and woman entered the hospital foyer, plainly agitated and in a hurry. The man was boisterous; his every movement seemed exaggerated. He went straight to the information desk, demanding something, wanting to know what was going on. The admitting clerk hushed him with waves of her hand and leaned forward gingerly to speak, to offer information perhaps. The man listened, squint-eyed, his mouth poised for quick rebuttal or contradiction. He did not want to listen. He had things to say. He began to argue, pacing about like a man who had demands to make.

The woman with him stepped back a little, giving him room—a slender, attractive woman, a pleasant contrast to the man. She wore a rust-colored pantsuit, slightly tailored, sophisticated, with a crisp, flared jacket. After a moment she went to the man, gently touching his arm, saying something. He waved her off, still talking to the woman behind the desk. She answered him with low, clipped phrases, then looked away, at her papers, apparently dismissing him.

"I know him," said Jerry, leaning forward attentively.

"What?"

"That man. He's Ronnie Mayhew's father."

"What's he doing here?"

"I'll find out." Jerry went to Mr. Mayhew and pumped his hand, talking quietly, soberly, to both the man and the woman. After a moment, he brought them back to Rachel.

"This is my wife, Rachel," he said, as Rachel stood

up and extended her hand. "Rachel, Darryl Mayhew. And Mrs. Mayhew."

"Karen," said the woman politely.

"How do you do?"

"I understand they've got your boy here too," boomed Darryl Mayhew.

"Yes," said Rachel.

"Ronnie's here, but I can't find out a thing. Those blasted nurses are as close-mouthed as corpses."

"Do you know what happened, why they're here?" asked Rachel anxiously.

"How in blazes would I know what happened? We drove down here from North Hollywood, left an important social engagement right in the middle of things. I'll have the devil to pay for that, I tell you. Money, contracts—it's costing me. But I'm here now and I want answers."

"We're waiting, too," said Jerry.

"We got a call from our neighbor," said Karen Mayhew. "She told me the police were at our house tonight and took several young people away, some to jail, she believed, and some to the hospital. She said she thought they brought Ronnie here."

"He is here, then?" asked Rachel.

"Yes, he's here," she replied. "Darryl just signed a treatment form or something; what did she call it, Darryl? Anyway, the nurse said we have to wait."

"They were at your house?" said Jerry, a baffled tone in his voice. "Your place?"

"Yes, it seems so," said Karen.

Jerry frowned. "Did you know that Brian took an overdose of drugs tonight?"

"Drugs?" repeated Karen Mayhew dully. "I don't

169

think Ronnie was going to have drugs at his little party. Not drugs."

"Listen, Webber, don't start again on that stuff about my kid on drugs. If your kid took an overdose, that's his problem. He's probably responsible for this whole stinking mess. If you think I like the police butting in on my business, disrupting everything, causing a ruckus, I tell you—"

While Darryl Mayhew stormed, Rachel's attention was turned to something else. Down the corridor came two men with hefty, robust frames. They seemed angry, or was it just purposeful? Even before they spoke, Rachel recognized that they were police detectives. They were coming with answers or with questions—or both.

Chapter Twenty-Three

The two policemen, dressed in plain dark suits, introduced themselves and showed their badges. Rachel looked away, listening only to their smooth clipped words, like a recording, all memorized.

They explained what happened that evening. Someone in the neighborhood had reported a disturbance at the Mayhew house. In checking it out, the police found a house full of stoned teenagers, all high on drugs. One boy was unconscious, apparently overdosed on barbiturates. Several youngsters were clumsily trying to wake him up, dragging him around; it was useless. They said his name was Brian Webber; he was only 13. This was his first time to get high on anything stronger than pot, and it was too much for him.

Another boy, in trying to escape, had crashed through a sliding glass door. He was bleeding badly and needed some stitches in his head. His name was Ronnie Mayhew and he was freaked out on amphetamines. Both Mayhew and the Webber boy had been rushed to the hospital. They were being treated now in the emergency room. Finishing the account of the incident, they explained that they had a few questions of their own. One of them, a Sergeant Hindman, turned to Mr. Mayhew and asked, "Where were you this evening, sir?"

"I was at a party, an important business function," blustered Darryl Mayhew. "It was imperative that I attend."

"Were you aware that your son was having a party at your home?"

"I knew he was having a few friends in. I saw nothing wrong with that."

"Were there any arrangements for a chaperone?"

"No. My son's 15. I trusted him."

"Did you have any idea that your son had drugs in his possession?"

"No, no," said Mayhew indignantly. "It was the Webber boy; he had the drugs. Ask his father if he didn't have the drugs. He told me so."

"Brian had some marijuana cigarettes. He said they belonged to a friend," replied Jerry evenly.

"Do you know what we found at your house tonight, Mr. Mayhew?" The sergeant's voice was crisp, restrained. "Are you familiar with bennies, dexies, goofballs, yellow-jackets, red devils, rainbows?"

"Those are drugs, pills—"

"Yes, pep pills—amphetamines, Benzedrine, Dexedrine. And barbiturates, downers, depressants, whatever you want to call them—Seconal, Phenobarbital, Nembutal. Every kid in your house had pills on him—and marijuana. Lots of marijuana cigarettes."

"And evidently they raided your liquor cabinet, too, Mr. Mayhew," added the other policeman dourly. "Several of the boys had liquor on their breath."

"That's a lethal combination, Mr. Mayhew, Mr. Webber," warned Sergeant Hindman. "Alcohol and pills, that's bad, real bad."

"Will Ronnie be all right?" asked Karen Mayhew earnestly.

"You'll have to check with the doctor, Mrs. Mayhew."

"What about Brian?" said Rachel.

"I don't know. You'll have to wait for the doctor."

"But you said he was unconscious."

"The doctor will talk with you," replied Sergeant Hindman firmly but kindly.

"Yes, thank you," said Rachel uncertainly.

"You understand, of course, that we'll have to question both boys as soon as they're able to answer," said the sergeant, offering his hand to say goodbye.

"We'll be in touch with you," said the other officer.

"The boys are in bad trouble, aren't they?" snapped Darryl Mayhew. "I suppose Ronnie'll have to go to court; there'll be a scandal. Am I right? Just tell me that. Am I right?"

"Perhaps for now you should just worry about getting the boys out of the hospital and on their feet again," suggested the sergeant. "Good night, Mr. and Mrs. Mayhew, Mr. and Mrs. Webber."

"We're in for it now, Karen," warned Darryl Mayhew hotly, when the policemen had gone. "I tell you, we're in for it. Those cops don't say anything; they can't tell you a thing. But I know, we're in for it."

"What are we going to do, Darryl?" asked Karen feebly, her hands fluttering like white wounded birds.

"I'll tell you what I'm going to do. I'm going to kill that boy," he growled. "I'll beat him to a pulp. He can't do this to me. I've given him everything he could ask for, everything. Did I ever say no when he asked for money, when he wanted to do something? Did I ever once say no? And this is how he repays me!"

Karen Mayhew turned sadly to Rachel. "I was afraid something like this would happen. Ronnie acted funny sometimes. I looked for drugs but I couldn't find anything. I looked. What else could I do?"

Rachel nodded mechanically. She was in a daze. She had heard too many words and nothing made sense. It was too much for her, too much to absorb. Her body and mind felt weighed down, heavy, like a great rock falling to the earth. She had to go back and sit down, quickly.

"Dear, you look so tired," said Karen Mayhew. "Your baby is due soon, isn't it?"

"Yes, in a month. I should sit down."

The woman made a helpless gesture as if to ease Rachel somehow; then with a baffled shrug, she joined Rachel on the couch. Next to this woman Rachel felt awkward and ugly and elephantine, a gross shapeless mass beside a lovely, fortyish sophisticate. Rachel's dress was a rumpled mess. The baby pounded inside her, twisting, squirming. He was pulling her down, pressing her down, so that she might never get up again. And Brian. Oh, God, what of Brian?

Then as she stared down the hall, her gaze fleeting and unfocused, a lanky dark-haired man came out of a room and stopped to speak a moment with a nurse, apparently concurring with her on some problem. He looked grimly toward Rachel, surveying the four of them in a glance, appraising them, a curious, impersonal gaze. Finally, he walked toward them, a sober, self-assured stride.

"Mr. and Mrs. Webber? Mr. and Mrs. Mayhew?"

"Yes," said Jerry. "Doctor—?"

"Yes, I'm Dr. Whalen."

"It's about time," said Darryl Mayhew loudly. "I want to know about Ronnie."

"You're Mr. Mayhew?"

"Yes. How is my son?"

"He's been taken to his room in the medical wing, Mr. Mayhew. He had some ugly facial cuts, but he's going to be all right. We'll have to keep him here a few days for observation."

"Can we see him?" asked Karen Mayhew, rubbing her hands together nervously. "Please let us see him."

"All right, just for a moment. Check with the nurse at the desk for his room number." He paused, apparently drawing his words together carefully. With a deliberate attempt at casualness, he said, "Oh, and Mr. and Mrs. Mayhew, it's too late to do anything tonight perhaps, but I would suggest you contact your family physician sometime tomorrow. Your son has a drug problem. But then I'm sure you realize that by now."

Glaring momentarily at the doctor, Darryl Mayhew pivoted and stalked off down the hall, muttering something, his eyes malicious slits in his puffy, reddened face. Karen Mayhew clattered softly after him in her neat, expensive black stacked heels. Shrugging her slight shoulders helplessly, she turned her head and mumbled something back at them. The words scattered and fell on the air, and no one understood her. Rachel smiled wanly and Dr. Whalen nodded politely and was still nodding when Rachel asked about Brian.

Averting his eyes, Dr. Whalen carefully steered a chair over to the couch and sat down. Jerry sat down beside Rachel, circling her shoulder with his arm. "How is Brian?" he asked anxiously, no longer masking his concern.

"You know your son took an overdose of barbiturates."

"Yes. Sergeant Hindman told us. Is he going to be all right?"

"Your son also had alcohol tonight, Mr. Webber. Do you know what that means?"

"Not exactly," said Jerry.

"We have what we call a 'synergistic effect.' That means that we must deal not only with the effects of alcohol and barbiturates but also with the effects of that combination."

"I don't understand," said Rachel, shaking her head dazedly.

"I don't think going into medical terms would help at this point, Mrs. Webber. It's enough that you know alcohol and barbiturates are a deadly combination. Your son has a fight on his hands."

"A fight? What do you mean, a fight?" demanded Jerry. "Is Brian aware of what's happened? Is he in pain? When can we see him?"

"Your son has been taken to the intensive care unit, Mr. Webber."

"Intensive care?"

Rachel stared at him.

There was a sad logical sound to the doctor's voice as he said, "Your son is in a coma. Presently he is breathing by mechanical means. We have him on a respirator. Our problem is to get him breathing on his own again."

"When can we see him?" said Jerry.

Dr. Whalen stood up. "I'll take you to him now."

Mutely Jerry and Rachel followed the doctor down the hall to the intensive care unit. Words were pounding inside Rachel's skull as she entered the room and approached Brian's bedside. *Coma. Respirator.* The words were going to explode inside her mind and scatter her senses all over the polished floor of the room.

Instead, her mind went blank as she saw Brian. He was deathly pale, smothered by a forbidding array of tubes and machinery. His bare, angular chest rose and fell with the gushing sound of the respirator, and his soft, boyish face was beaded with perspiration. A shot of darkness cut off Rachel's vision, then brought it back again with a flash like lightning. She swayed; her body was folding up like spaghetti. She was going down, down.

"Are you all right, Mrs. Webber?" asked Dr. Whalen with concern.

Rachel shook her head, clearing it. "Yes, yes, I'm all right. But Brian. Dr. Whalen—?"

Jerry interrupted, supporting Rachel with his arm. "Dr. Whalen, when do you think Brian will start breathing on his own and come out of the coma?"

The doctor cleared his throat, a professional, calculated cough as he steered them away from the bedside. "Very soon we hope. The sooner the better. We're doing everything possible." He shifted his gaze—a certain restless gesture, as if this conversation were something he would like to dismiss. He walked with them back to the lobby, then turned to Jerry and said, "On the forms you signed, you listed Dr. Richard Quinn as your family physician. He has been contacted and will probably be here shortly. There really isn't much else I can tell you now."

"But Brian will be all right? He will start breathing again, won't he?" insisted Rachel, a terrible panic writhing up through her chest, suffocating her. "He will come out of the coma sooner or later."

The doctor's face was an inscrutable mask.

"He will be all right, won't he?" repeated Rachel.

The doctor offered a forlorn smile. "We'll do everything we can, Mrs. Webber."

What else did the doctor say? His words were like thick, jumbled soup. Rachel was drowning in his words: she couldn't breathe. His words were fragments, knocking her down.

Rachel could not recall the doctor leaving. He had told her to go home and get some sleep. When she refused, he told Jerry to go get some strong black coffee. It would be good for them, he said. Jerry was getting the coffee. And the doctor went off somewhere, perhaps back to take care of Brian. Rachel didn't see him go.

The coffee was too hot and scorched Rachel's throat. Her throat burned. It felt raw. She kept drinking, drinking the coffee down, holding the styrofoam cup to her lips until the black liquid was gone. It burned down through her chest into her stomach. At least it was making her feel something.

She and Jerry sat together for hours. It seemed like hours. It wasn't really. Or perhaps it was. She would not go home. Perhaps someone would come with news. Perhaps Brian would wake and call for her, wanting her that instant. She would wait. She drank more coffee and made frequent trips down the hall to the ladies' room, where she inspected her pale face in the mirror beneath the fluorescent lights. She was a ghost, with a vivid white sheen on her face and eerie shadows under her eyes. Her eyes were wide, unblinking, frightened birds' eyes.

The contractions that were a familiar part of Rachel's days lately were increasing noticeably tonight. The gradual tightening across her hardened abdomen, was no longer merely a passing discomfort; it was becoming pain, demanding her attention. Rachel told herself that this happened when she was especially tired. Tonight she was extremely tired. She had been up all night. It was nearly four in the morning.

Jerry insisted again that she go home. No, no, she would stay. She put her head on his shoulder, nearly dozing once or twice. He rubbed the back of her neck and her shoulders. Her back ached; her head ached. He rubbed her forehead and then went somewhere to find her some aspirin. When he came back, he sat and prayed with her, talking to her with tender, soothing words. She had a New Testament with Psalms in her purse, and he took it and read to her.

While he read, she thought a lot about death. Christ died; her beloved Christ. She thought of that. The Lord Himself died for her, for Jerry, for Brian. Brian knew Christ, she was sure of that. If Brian died, he would be in God's presence. He would be with Christ, perhaps this very night.

Once while Jerry rubbed her shoulders, she murmured, "What if Brian dies?" She couldn't recall what Jerry said. Did he answer? What did he say? Jerry read from the Psalms. Jerry prayed, talking out loud. His voice was soft, a gentle melody. Rachel listened, nodding, murmuring yes, yes. She loved God; she loved Jerry. Somehow, within her grief there was a harmony, a comforting awareness of God's presence. Even now, God was present. Blessed Christ.

Before dawn, around 5 or 5:30, Rachel was aware of something new. A feeling within her belly, a jagged, sudden lurching of something solid inside her. An involuntary reflex of actual pain. Rachel gasped and sat up straight. "What is it?" said Jerry.

"Nothing. The baby's kicking," cried Rachel, still feeling the pain.

"Are you sure?"

Rachel held her body still, waiting, listening, aware of the intricate function of all the parts of her body. Everything was working together, a quiet inner pounding, a steady flow of juices through the network of arteries and veins beneath her skin, the harmony of bones and tissue and muscle and blood. But now there was more. Pain—!

She pressed the flat of her hand against her abdomen on the spot that she knew to be the baby's back. She waited, breathless, for his response. Whenever she nudged him, he moved; he always moved. It was like a game, this gentle nudging and his immediate reflex. Bump him; he bumped back. Nudge. There was nothing. She pressed again, harder. She waited. Nothing. Again! Nothing. Her baby was still. Again she pressed, urgently, demanding a response. Only pain, racing into the myriad cells of her body.

Aloud, to her husband, she said, "Something's wrong with the baby. He doesn't move. I can't feel him move. He's dead, Jerry. I think my baby's dead!"

Chapter Twenty-Four

It was peculiar, this feeling, this sensation. It was too much, thought Rachel. It was taking over. The simple fact was that there was a baby inside her struggling to be born. He would not stop until he saw the light of day. He was more real now than she, this baby, his body more real than her own. It was his show. He was in charge now.

This baby had to live. She could not stand it if this baby were not alive. She could not stand to have a dead baby inside her struggling to be born.

Rachel's mind was ponderous, confused. What was going on? People came and went, doing things for her, to her. They all looked busy, these people in their white, impersonal outfits. They were too busy to talk; they did their business without a word.

"Put your clothes in this closet," a nurse told her finally. Obediently she undressed and put her clothing away and slipped into the coarse hospital gown. She got up into the large, sturdy bed and covered herself with a sheet, waiting for whatever would happen next.

"The doctor will be here soon to examine you," the same nurse said, buzzing around the room as if she had a great many duties to perform and would get all of them out of the way as efficiently as possible. She slung a contraption around Rachel's arm, tightened it, and took her blood pressure. "Just relax, Hon, you'll be okay," the nurse said blandly.

Rachel was grateful for this kind word from a busy nurse. It was more than she expected. Somehow it helped to clear her mind, to focus her thoughts upon her immediate situation. She found the courage to ask, "But my baby, my baby isn't due for a month yet. Since I came up here I haven't felt him move—not a kick or anything."

The nurse breezed out of the room and returned swiftly with a stethoscope which she placed over several areas of Rachel's bulging abdomen, pausing each time to listen, a mild cryptic expression on her face.

"Baby has a good heartbeat," she said matter-of-factly, and was gone. She returned moments later with pills in a small paper cup. "These will help you relax," she explained. "You're tighter than a drum. Try to get some rest now."

Rachel swallowed the pills and returned the cup to the nurse's waiting hand. Before the nurse could turn on her heel to leave, Rachel managed to ask, "Where is my husband? Will I be able to see him?"

The nurse was at the door by the time she answered. "I imagine he's down the hall in the expectant father's waiting room. When we have you ready, he can come and stay with you until it's time for the baby to come."

"I'm glad. Thank you." Then, lifting herself on one elbow, she asked anxiously, "Nurse, I was wondering, have you heard anything about my son . . . any word?"

The nurse's crisp expression changed subtly, softening perhaps, but Rachel couldn't quite interpret the change. Shaking her head stiffly, she said, "No, no, I'm sorry. I don't know anything about your son."

And she was gone.

Later, Jerry appeared in the doorway, looking weary and disheveled as he approached her bedside. Rachel pulled herself into a sitting position and let her legs dangle over the side of the bed so that she could face him while they talked. She had the fleeting impression that it had been days since she had last seen him, not merely two hours. There was a small, fretful smile on his lips that turned up the corners of his mouth like hooks, a smile that no doubt mirrored Rachel's own brittle expression.

"How are you?" he asked.

"All right. I don't feel too bad, considering."

"You scared me to death. I thought we were going to lose the baby."

Rachel's smile was splintered, inside out. "I thought so too."

"But he's okay?"

The smile righted itself and softened perceptibly. "The nurse heard his heartbeat. He has a good strong heartbeat. She said so."

"That's wonderful."

Rachel glanced down sheepishly at her gown, at her own swollen body that turned the gown into a pale, humorless balloon. "I look so terrible," she complained self-consciously.

"No, you look beautiful. Like a lovely madonna."

"You haven't said that for a long time. Madonna. I thought you forgot."

"No," he said, hovering over her attentively. He patted her knee with an awkward hand; then, as she relaxed, he rubbed the calf of her leg gently, soothingly. "I'm remembering more all the time, Rae. I'm remembering how much I love you."

She grinned foolishly. "I love you too."

"That makes me very happy, Rachel."

She smiled into his eyes, feeling lighter somehow, almost pleased, as if they had come through some sort of trial. What was it? A process of learning to respond to each other again? It seemed to Rachel like an important moment, but she had no words to make it tangible, so instead, she tucked the corners of her gown around her thighs and said, "This thing doesn't even have a back, Jerry. A backless gown. How about that?"

He squeezed her knee, smiling, his lips closed in a perfect arc. "It looks fine, fine," he said.

Laughing lightly, Rachel patted his hand. "You do a lot for my confidence, Darling."

Gently changing the subject, he asked, "Do you really feel all right, Rae? Has the doctor been to see you yet?"

"No, but they called him. He'll be here," she said reassuringly. She wound the corner of the sheet around her finger, making a very neat bandage. In the silence of the room she unwound it, pressing the curl out flat. "Jerry," she said, after a moment.

"Yes, Honey?"

"You haven't said anything about Brian."

His eyes were suddenly grim, his expression distracted. "There's nothing new. I went in to see him, but he looks the same."

She persisted, twisting the sheet again into a ragged knot. "But you will tell me as soon as there's any change—even if it's bad. You will tell me, even if I'm in labor, no matter what."

Acquiescing, he mumbled, "I'll tell you as soon as I find out anything, anything at all."

"Thank you, Jerry. I had to know that."

"I know."

Feeling a sudden exhaustion sweep over her, Rachel pulled her legs up under the sheets and lay back. "I'm so tired, Jerry." She tried to smile at him. "They gave me something so I could relax."

"Why don't you try to sleep, Darling?" He pulled a chair over to the bed, dragging it along the floor, so that it made a scraping sound. He sat down heavily and offered her a smile. "I'll sit right here," he said. "I'll be right here all the time."

Rachel slept until noon, when her obstetrician, Dr. Bernard Oberg, came to examine her. Jerry stepped out for a breath of fresh air and a quick cup of coffee from the vending machine, returning only after the doctor had completed the examination.

"How is she?" Jerry asked when the two men met in the hall.

Dr. Oberg was a quietly jovial man, tall and limber, with a shock of red hair that made him look a beguiling 30 instead of a settled 40. With a candid grin, he said, "She's doing fine, Mr. Webber, just fine."

"And the baby?"

"The baby's taking his own sweet time, so she has a while to wait yet. Since the baby's premature, the muscles are tight, so it's going to take a little work on Rachel's part."

Jerry spoke over the strain in his voice. "Will the baby be all right, being premature and all?"

Rubbing his chin thoughtfully, the doctor said, "I really don't see why not. I'd guess the baby is over five pounds. I don't anticipate any problems."

"Good, good," sighed Jerry, sinking his hands into

his trouser pockets in a gesture of relief. "She hasn't had much rest, Doctor. Did you hear about our son?"

The doctor shot Jerry an earnest glance, frowning. "Yes, I heard. I'm sorry."

Jerry shrugged helplessly. "Well, Rachel was up all night. I tried to get her to go home, but you know how it is. I just want this to be as easy for her as possible; do you know what I mean?"

"I understand, Mr. Webber. Does Intensive Care know where you are?"

"Yes, I told them," Jerry replied.

Rachel was sitting up in bed eating lunch when Jerry entered the labor room again. They exchanged warm smiles.

"What's this? Breakfast in bed?" he teased gently.

"Lunch. But it's terrible. Look. Clear tea, bouillon, plain jello. I could eat a steak."

"They don't want you to have any food in your stomach."

"I know. But even a cracker—"

"How are the contractions?"

"Not too bad. They hurt, but I can handle it. But I'm getting impatient, I'm afraid. I want things to hurry up."

Jerry sat down in the chair by her bed and stretched out his legs. "I know, Baby. I saw Dr. Oberg out in the hall."

She nodded. "Yes, I heard you. He told me I'm dilated to three, but the baby won't be born until I'm at ten."

Jerry looked puzzled. "Do you understand that?"

"I understand I have seven to go, and that's too much. I want to get this over with."

"Try to be patient, Hon."

Rachel sipped her tea. It was too hot. She poured

186

some water into it from the glass on her bedstand. "I'll try, Jerry," she answered half-heartedly. She ate her jello but had no appetite for the bouillon. Pushing away her tray, she said, "I was going to be all ready, Jerry. I have all these books at home on natural childbirth. I was even thinking of taking a class—"

"You'll do fine, Darling, fine."

"But I want to be ready," she insisted. "This is too soon; I don't know if I can do it. I'm so tired; I don't even want to think about it, Jerry. I just want it over."

He reached for her hand and kissed it. "Soon, Darling, soon."

During the afternoon, Rachel was aware that the contractions were gradually increasing in frequency and intensity. Finally, they were something she could no longer shrug off or ignore. Her body hardened against the pain, fighting it. Trying to relax, trying to think of other things, Rachel would stare at the ceiling and rub against the hardness of her abdomen with her fingertips. Her thoughts kept coming back to this, her baby, the imminence of his birth. There was no turning back. She had to ride this one all the way. It would get worse before it got better.

"You're not relaxing," accused Jerry softly, rubbing her arm.

"What?"

"You're stiff. You're fighting it."

"It hurts."

"I know enough to know you should relax. Try to relax, Baby. Let your arms go limp. Don't fight it."

"I'm trying," she whispered huskily.

Late in the afternoon, Dr. Oberg came again to check Rachel and informed her in his soft cheerful voice that it would be soon now. She was dilated to seven, he said. Almost at transition. Another hour perhaps, or maybe longer. He asked if she wanted some medication for the discomfort. Shaking her head vigorously, she said, "No, Doctor. It's better for the baby if I don't have a lot of stuff to dope me up, isn't that right? Didn't I read that somewhere?"

"It's possible, Rachel," he answered in a noncommittal voice.

"Especially for a premature baby?" persisted Rachel.

"I suppose. But it's important for you to be comfortable too, to save your strength and energy."

"I don't want anything, Dr. Oberg. No anesthetic, please. Nothing."

He patted her arm soothingly, as if she were a temperamental child he wished to appease without actually giving in to her demands. "We'll see when the time comes," he said mildly. "Then if you want a saddle-block, fine. If not, and you seem to be doing all right, then perhaps we'll just give you a local anesthetic for the episiotomy."

Rachel flashed him a hopeful smile. "I just want to do everything I can for my baby."

"Of course you do," Dr. Oberg replied cheerfully.

During the next hour, to forget the pain, Rachel forced her mind to go over all the events in her life since she found out she was pregnant. Like going over ancient photographs in an old family album, the events were etched in her brain, blending together, sometimes fuzzy, unfocused, with swirling blacks and whites or soft, blurring colors, strung out in her thoughts, obliterating the cramps, the pain. Photographs. Make them work. Make them happen. One by one. Brian. Jerry. Jerry moving out of the house because he was involved with a girl named Kit. Jerry's face, the agony, the hurt when he left. Brian's face, the disappointment. Better to recall these memories than to think of the pain now; better, better. Fragments of memory. A possible divorce. Problems with Brian.

It all seemed unreal now, as if her life had happened to someone else, someone Rachel hardly knew, a stranger. Now all of these things were part of the past. As the pain increased, Rachel could no longer summon the images clearly. All the events of her life were stuck somewhere in her brain like bits of shrapnel, out of sight. Nothing surfaced, nothing was clear, but everything was there, hidden, stabbing her consciousness, unrelenting.

Cramps. Waves and waves of cramps knocked her down. If only she could ride with them, stay on top. She was always washed under, left gasping for breath, and befuddled by a wilderness of pain. It seemed to Rachel that she was being swallowed up; spiritually, mentally, physically, she was being consumed. Something more than the baby attacked her, bombarding her will. Her strength was draining away, gone. Her body was a broken dam, ready to spill out its contents and leave her with nothing, empty. Her mind was used up and flying into the wind like confetti. Where was everything going to end? Where? When? Or had it ended already? Was this the final breaking apart, the ultimate destruction of Rachel Webber?

Chapter Twenty-Five

"You're doing fine, Rae." This a voice miles away, an unreal voice, dreamy.

"Jerry?"

"I'm right here, Baby."

"It's getting bad, really bad."

"Should I call the nurse? She could get you something."

"No, no. I don't want anything. I'm all right. I just wish I could remember those breathing techniques. Breathing is important, did you know? I don't think I'm breathing right."

"Just relax, Baby," said Jerry soothingly. He rubbed her forehead, stroking gently. "That's it, relax."

"Why don't we hear something about Brian?" asked Rachel plaintively, irritation stealing into her voice. "Why don't they tell us something?"

"The doctor knows where we are," replied Jerry softly. "He said he'd let us know if there's any change at all."

Taking Jerry's hand in hers, Rachel hugged it against her breast. "Jerry, Jerry, if Brian dies, I don't want to live either."

"You don't mean that, Rachel."

"I don't know. I can't imagine living without Brian. How could things ever be the same again?"

"They couldn't," said Jerry simply. He leaned his face close to hers so that his mouth was near her cheek. "Rachel, Rachel," he said tenderly, "this is the moment when we have to trust the Lord, don't you see that? Not with words, Baby, but with our hearts, our souls. If we don't trust Him now, we may never really trust Him again with anything. This is the test of what we are, what we have, what we believe. Listen, Baby, we have hope. Rachel, we hold on to the hope of Christ!"

Rachel's breath was short, hardly there. She murmured, "Which hope we have as an anchor of the soul, both sure and steadfast—"

"Is that from the Bible?"

"Yes. Somewhere . . . . I believe it, Jerry, what that verse says. I do. I hold to the hope of Christ. I want to, Jerry."

"It's something Christ has given us, Rachel. Hope. Cling to it; it keeps everything else in perspective."

Closing her eyes and licking the dryness from her lips, Rachel quoted prayerfully, "Therefore my heart is glad, and my glory rejoiceth; my flesh also shall rest in hope."

Jerry caressed her head, her hair. "Yes, yes, Darling, that's good. That has to be our stand, yes."

"Therefore my heart is—" She stiffened suddenly, wrenching away from his caress.

"Rachel, what is it?"

"I feel different. Something's happening, Jerry. I have to push; I can't control it."

"I'll get someone!"

One nurse appeared, then another, scurrying into the room, checking, poking, listening with their stethoscopes, bustling about, twittering like quick, earnest birds. Jerry was quickly waved out of the room.

Rachel heard one nurse, a gangly, rawboned woman, exclaim loudly, "Where's Dr. Oberg? This baby's coming!"

"We paged him," someone said. "He's on his way up from the cafeteria."

A moment later, Dr. Oberg sauntered in with a confident smile and patted her hand. "We planned this one pretty well, Rachel. I just finished my coffee. How do you feel?"

"I have a terrible urge to push," she cried, panting, breathless. "I can't control it."

"Do you remember feeling that way with your other child?" he asked.

"It was so long ago. I think so, yes."

"Then you know you're in the final stage of labor, and your baby will be born very shortly."

"Yes, yes."

"You're doing fine, Rachel," he said. "We're taking you to the delivery room now. Have you decided about an anesthetic?"

"No. I mean, I don't want one. Just hurry, Doctor. Please!"

There was a blur of activity around Rachel. Nothing was clear or well-defined, for Rachel's senses were absorbed by the upheaval within her own body. It was a thing beyond her, gripping her, a stampede of her insides, as if a ton of pressure pummeled the walls of her flesh, plummeting, plunging! She was caught in the avalanche, losing control.

She was aware of movement, her bed being rolled into the hallway, down the hall. Just before her bed was pushed through the open doors into the delivery room, she caught a glimpse of Jerry standing in the hallway, watching, looking helpless. She said something that seemed a little crazy to her later: "If we had taken the natural childbirth classes, you could come in with me."

He waved her on encouragingly, with, "Next time, Rachel, next time!"

Then someone was rolling her onto another bed and covering her with sheets and putting her feet in stirrups. The doctor was saying something about not pushing yet. What? Was he kidding? It was beyond her control. Above her head was a huge, pale light like some sort of moon, out of focus, imaginary. A disc, wide and pervasive, was spraying soft light over the room. The nurses and doctors were busy, apparently unconcerned with her, doing things, obviously synchronized and working together expertly like the mechanical parts of a clock. Perfect precision. Their movements like rhythm, a delicate syncopation. They knew what they were doing.

But Rachel couldn't appreciate their expertise now. Suddenly she found herself bearing down with what was surely cataclysmic force. Did she have such power, such strength? She was turning herself inside out.

"Not yet, Rachel, not yet." The doctor's voice. He pointed to a mirror overhead in case she cared to watch. She looked away.

"Doctor, I—"

"All right, Rachel, on the next contraction, I want you to bear down . . . all right, now, now, Rachel!"

The waves of the sea slammed against rock, breaking it. . . .

"That's good, Rachel, good. You're doing fine. We have his head. See in the mirror, Rachel? Next his shoulders. A slight turn. Relax a moment, Rachel. Take a good breath. Yes. All right, on the next contraction, another good push. Okay, here it comes. Now push, Rachel, push."

Push, push, push!

Rachel heard a cry. Not her own voice, not her own agonized sigh. No. Her baby.

"A girl, Rachel, a girl!" cried Dr. Oberg, holding the child up by her feet so that Rachel could see the smooth, lithe, cheesy body of her daughter and the thick, purplish umbilical cord still attached, a remnant sign of their oneness.

"She looks fine, Rachel, just fine. Ten fingers, ten toes, everything in place," assured Dr. Oberg, with a light, easy laugh.

The nurses were already working with the child, cleaning mucus from her nose and mouth. Rachel could not see all that they did, but she heard the steady cry, the lovely, healthy cry of her baby. Within minutes, the nurses had her daughter in a small crib beside her, and while the doctor delivered the afterbirth and stitched the episiotomy, Rachel kept her eyes constantly on the small, thrashing, squealing infant at her side. Her darling child had fine downy black hair, a red face, and white, clinched fists, so delicate, so very tiny. Her feet kicked the air and her miniature belly heaved with sobs.

Over and over, Rachel whispered, "She's beautiful, beautiful, beautiful!"

Later, in the recovery room, Rachel could think of nothing but sleep. A nurse brought her graham crackers and apple juice, which Rachel devoured immediately. But, after that, she wanted only to succumb to her dreams. She was empty, and it was a warm, delicious feeling. Through the dregs of sleep she praised God, her

Savior, her Lord, the giver of life. Wonderful life.

Even when Jerry stole in to kiss her good night and tell her what a beautiful daughter she had given him, Rachel could offer no response except for a drowsy, contented smile. Then, gladly, she gave up her body and mind to sleep.

Chapter Twenty-Six

Rachel had the bed by the window. It was a two-bed room, but the other bed was empty, so for the present she would have privacy. It was morning. Someone had drawn back the curtains, and sunlight streamed into the room, turning the walls a warm, creamy yellow.

Blinking her eyes against the sun, Rachel pulled her tangled thoughts from the grogginess of slumber. She still had that warm, fuzzy feeling about her that comes from sound sleep. She could not quite distinguish the warm, languorous sections of her body from the cocoon warmth of blankets and sheets. She stretched, testing the separate parts of her body for pain and discomfort. Not too bad. No, not bad at all.

Within Rachel was a perfect silence, a hush, although she could hear the muted hospital sounds outside her room. Voices. Distant, insistent baby cries from the nursery down the hall. Carts wheeling about. The metallic clickety-clack of utensils and trays. Padded, purposeful footsteps. Sounds fading in and out, the constant, quiet hum of hospital noise. But within Rachel was a simple quiet. Peace.

She was ready for this day—Sunday, yes, Sunday. She was ready for whatever would come. For whatever news Jerry would bring. Ready. A wellspring of peace inside her smoothed out the jaggedness of anxiety and fear. She was not afraid.

She recalled a familiar verse. "Thou wilt keep him in perfect peace, whose mind is stayed on Thee: because he trusteth in Thee." Yes. No longer just words, but reality. Something to live by and hold on to, no matter what came. It was clear to her now: Jesus Christ was her reality. She owed Him her life, all that she was, all that she would ever be. It was a blessed, wonderful obligation, one which Jerry also shared, willingly, gladly. Together, no matter what happened, they would be all right; they would make it. Their priorities were in order.

And Brian, their son. Still a question mark. But God would have His way, and He would supply the grace. Still, oh, God, let Brian live, thought Rachel prayerfully. But more than that, more than that, Thy will be done!

Jerry showed up a few minutes after Rachel's breakfast tray had been removed. He still had the walk of a weary man, but his face was shaven and there was a special light in his eyes that Rachel recognized as his love for her. A lovely, welcome light, his love.

Rachel sat up in bed. "Jerry, what are you doing here?" she asked, feeling suddenly anxious. "Visiting hours aren't until this afternoon."

He gave her a quick kiss on the lips, then took both her hands in his. "I got special permission from the doctor, Darling."

She stared at him. "It's Brian, isn't it? You've come to tell me about Brian."

"Yes."

"Is he—?"

"He's better, Rachel. He started breathing on his own early this morning," said Jerry, rubbing his large hands over her vulnerable, small ones.

"Breathing? Then . . . then he's all right? He'll be all right?"

Jerry pulled her close to him and kissed her forehead and hair. "Darling," he said, "Brian is still in a coma, but the doctor says he has passed the crisis. We don't know how long the coma will last. He's not out of the woods yet. He has a long way to go, and we have a long way to go with him, but yes, I think he will be all right. I really do think he'll pull through."

"Thank God, Jerry. Oh, praise God!"

"You know, it could easily have gone the other way. He could have died."

"I know, I know." Pulling her head away from his chest and looking at him carefully, Rachel asked, "Have you seen him this morning, Jerry?"

"Yes, just for a few minutes. Of course, he didn't know I was there, but I sat by his bed holding his hand, just watching him. I suppose it was silly, but I even talked to him. I kept praying he might be able to hear me. I told him about the baby and said we were all going to be a family again. I even mentioned that we may move to Cleveland, where he can see his grandparents and have a house with a big yard."

"Oh, a house and a yard?"

"Sure, why not?" said Jerry. "Haven't you always wanted a home of our own and a nice yard where our children could play?"

Rachel smiled and hugged her husband. "Jerry, you know how I've wanted a home. It would be wonderful!"

"We'll have that and more. We'll have a Christian home, Darling."

Rachel studied her husband's face, trying to read his

expression. "Jerry, we are going to be all right, aren't we—all four of us?"

"I hope so, Darling. Of course, there will be things to deal with. Therapy for Brian, for the three of us. Showing him we're a family again, that we want to be a Christ-centered family. It will be difficult, Rachel. Brian may recover physically—I pray that he does. But how will he be emotionally and spiritually? We can't predict what scars he may have. We have to be ready to do everything possible to win Brian back. But, with the Lord's help, I believe we can do it."

"We must trust God for it," said Rachel soberly.

"I telephoned Marlene and Dr. Emrick and they're both praying. Dr. Emrick will be requesting prayer for Brian in the morning worship service," said Jerry. "By the way, Marlene will be over to see you right after church. She said Mr. Timmons will drive her," he added with a wink.

"I'm so glad," Rachel responded, reaching for her pink satin robe at the foot of the bed. She swung it around her shoulders. "The nurse gave me the suitcase you brought in this morning," she said, her fingers busy with the soft, quilted buttons of the robe.

"Good," replied Jerry. "I thought you would like having your own things—some nightgowns, a bathrobe, your toothbrush."

"Yes, thank you. My own things certainly are better than these sleazy hospital gowns."

"Yes, they are," he agreed, smiling. "Did I remember everything?"

"Yes, Jerry. Thank you." She paused a moment, then added, "And now it's time for me to get out of bed."

"Shouldn't you wait a while?" Jerry asked with a frown.

"No, you don't understand. They get you up right away. It's better for you. Really."

He laughed. "All right, if you say so. You're the expert in these matters."

A light broke in Rachel's eyes, as if something important had suddenly dawned on her, and she exclaimed, "Jerry, do you realize—?"

He looked up, startled. "What?"

"Can you believe it? I haven't even asked yet. Have you seen the baby, our baby?"

He grinned. "I certainly have. Would I miss that—our baby? Sure, I saw her. I stopped by the nursery right after seeing Brian."

"She's beautiful, isn't she? I mean, even if she is wrinkled and red."

"She's gorgeous. She looks like you—well, she will in time. She'll have the same slender neck and dark hair; she'll be another madonna—just like her mother."

"Do you realize we haven't even thought of a name for her yet?" said Rachel. "I mean, we can't call her Miss X for the rest of her life. She has to have a name."

"That's right. We have to have a name."

"I have one, Jerry," said Rachel.

"You do? What? What is it?"

"Hope."

"Hope?" he echoed thoughtfully. "Miss Hope Webber. Hope. Yes, you know, I like it. That's good."

"It's an appropriate name, Jerry."

"Yes, yes, it is."

Rachel touched Jerry's arm lightly with her fingertips. "I want to go see her, Jerry. Let's go down to the nursery together right now and see Miss Hope Webber and tell her she has a loving family waiting for her, waiting to take her home."

Jerry helped Rachel out of bed, supporting her with his arms until she was able to stand on her feet. "Rae," he said, watching her protectively, "are you sure it won't be too long a walk for you?"

"Oh, no," she cried. "It will be a wonderful walk. But I need you beside me. I'm still a little clumsy on my feet. You see? I have to lean on you."

Rachel put her arm around Jerry's shoulder and leaned happily against him. "Okay, I'm ready," she said, smiling.

He kissed her once gently. Then, circling her waist with his arm, he led her out of the room and down the hall to the nursery, where Hope was waiting.